You Matter To God

A Book Of Sermons

You Matter To God

A Book Of Sermons

Larry Monroe Arrowood

You Matter To God
A Book Of Sermons

Larry Monroe Arrowood

Copyright © Pending 2020

All rights reserved.

Scripture quotations are from THE KING JAMES VERSION OF THE BIBLE (KJV) unless otherwise noted.

Some Scripture quotations are from THE HOLY BIBLE, NEW INTERNATIONAL VERSION® NIV® Copyright © 1973, 1978, 1984 by International Bible Society®
Used by permission. All rights reserved worldwide.

Woodsong Publishing
5989 Spring Meadow Lane
Seymour, IN 47274

You may purchase additional books written by Larry Arrowood from the Woodsong Publishing website or through your preferred booksellers. See the back of this book for additional titles by the author.

www.woodsongpublishing.com
woodsongpublishing@yahoo.com

Cover design by Vision Graphics, Seymour, IN
Printed in the United States of America

ISBN: 978-1-7349323-4-8

Contents

Dedication	6
Introduction	7
You Matter	9
A Mistake To Avoid	21
Dealing With Our Sins	31
Do You Want To Be Made Whole	39
Forgiveness	49
Mercy Is Not Approval	59
Inject A Little Madness	73
Is There Not A Cause	81
Memento Mori: Remember To Die	87
No More Shame	95
Our Spiritual Defense System	105
Renewing The Mind	111
Jesus The Giver: Satan The Taker	119
Suffering With Purpose	129
That All May Know	139
The Banyan Tree	149
The Lord Always Has Another Move	157
Monotheism	167
The Story Of Dawson Springs	179
The Zeal Of The Lord	189
There Will Come A Day	203
This I Know	213
Time To Come Home	229
When We Talk To Ourselves	237
You Can Do This	245

Dedication

To my sons, Andrew and Aaron, who are pastors

To my Grandsons,
Matthew who is a licensed minister
Zion who desires ministry

To my sisters Joyce, Sue, and Sherry who are married to ministers

To my Dad who answered the call of ministry in his latter years and founded a church in Florence, KY

To my Grandpa, affectionately know as Preacher Charlie, who ministered in the Appalachian region of Eastern Kentucky

Introduction

What's in a sermon? As "No man is an island, entire of itself,"[1] most sermons are not the creation of a singular speaker. They are a compilation of some God thoughts, along with references, discussions, and a whole lot of borrowing from other's ideas, especially in this Age of Internet.

I've borrowed many a sermon idea, and some have probably made it into this book. It's tough for ministers to remember if their thoughts came from the Bible or a buddy. We like to credit sermon ideas as Divine inspiration, when some sermons simply come from another source. Here's how that works: Both of my sons are pastors, so we often discuss our weekly sermons. This sometimes equates to preaching each others' sermons—with a little personal touch-up. And when a fresh sermon thought eludes a minister—not to mention it's thirty minutes before the Sunday service—borrowing a sermon is a temptation hard to resist. That's why, hopefully without being presumptuous, I give my permission for you to preach any or all of these sermons. My only request: improve them for me.

I hope this compilation of sermons helps someone. I'm honored you'd read them. I'll be doubly honored if you take one of the thoughts to the pulpit or to a Sunday School class or to a small study group and give it another chance to encourage a life I can never touch. Thanks for reading and kindest regards!

Larry Arrowood

Endnote
1) John Donne's Devotions, 1624

You Matter

One of his disciples, Andrew, Simon Peter's brother, saith unto him, There is a lad here, which hath five barley loaves, and two small fishes: but what are they among so many? And Jesus took the loaves; and when he had given thanks, he distributed to the disciples, and the disciples to them that were set down; and likewise of the fishes as much as they would. When they were filled, he said unto his disciples, Gather up the fragments that remain, that nothing be lost. Therefore they gathered them together, and filled twelve baskets with the fragments of the five barley loaves, which remained over and above unto them that had eaten.

John 6:8-13

Jesus, on several occasions, tried to stretch the apostles' faith. After His departure from the earth, He needed men who would believe Him in impossible situations, for He was asking them to do the unthinkable: twelve men would head up the task of taking the gospel message to the entire world. When we see the apostles huddled in fear after Christ's crucifixion, we wonder if they could ever be a winning team. But with God, nothing is impossible; however, we must keep God in the equation. Too often we don't; rather, we go it alone. Here's the contrast in trusting God or not:

- With God, Simon Peter walked on the surface of the raging Galilee, but on his own, like a rock skipping

across the surface of a lake, he lost momentum and began to sink.
- When young David trusted in God, he defeated Goliath with a stone and a sling, ultimately winning a significant victory over the apposing army. Later, when he trusted in his own strength and numbered the men of Israel to determine the power of his army, he caused the death of 70,000 Israelites.
- On his own, Jonah was a pitiful sight: cowering in the corner of a sinking ship, tossed with the luggage over the ship's handrail, gulped down by a huge fish, and finally wallowing in the bilge of the fish's stomach. But when he surrendered to God, he became a thundering voice that brought the masses to their knees.

From beginning to end, our Christian walk is a journey of faith. The writer of Hebrews expressed, "… without faith it is impossible to please him …" (Hebrews 11:6). Some are overwhelmed by this concept because they view faith as some humongous quality of spirituality which only a select few can acquire: Moses, Daniel, and Paul as examples. We can become forlorn as we compare ourselves with heroes of Scripture, wondering how they became such spiritual giants. The problem? We have emphasized the qualities of the Bible characters instead of the qualities of the God of the Bible.

No doubt, David was a brave lad and excellent with a sling. Samson's will was as powerful as his forearms and triceps. But their accomplishments were through God, not their personal abilities.

You Matter

When we place the emphasis in the wrong place, God is sidelined, and victory becomes elusive. To advance God's Kingdom, we must incorporate biblical faith, for meaningful victories aren't accomplished apart from faith, no matter how resourceful we may be. Faith is not about man's ability, talent, intellect, or any of his personal qualities. Faith is about trusting in the all-sufficient God of the Bible: something even a child can do.

Let me try and simplify the definition of faith. On a trip to the Mediterranean, my son Aaron purchased for me a unique gift: a small, ornate clock. I say unique because both the front and the back are glass. Not only can I see the hands turning in the front, but likewise, from the backside, I can see the gears working in harmony to produce the rhythmic tic-tic of the second hand. Since this clock was a manual wind up, and I am not accustomed to such, I accidentally wound the gears too tightly—not to mention my son purchased the clock at a tourist trap. Trying to fix my mistake, I unscrewed the front glass and attempted to manually "unwind" the clock; however, instead of fixing my previous error, I broke the minute and hour hands. So, I now have this unique, ornate clock, wound so tightly that the gears are frozen in place. And even if the gears worked, there are no minute and hour hands to reveal the time.

This broken clock can be a description of faith. Just as a broken clock doesn't affect time, neither does our limited understanding of God prevent Him from being God. As time existed before there was a clock, God existed before time. Time does not prove or disprove God: God created time. There was never a time when He did not exist; there will never be a time when He ceases to exist. When time as we know it has ceased, God will still be God, and His eternity (timelessness) shall begin.

Faith is not what we see. Faith is what we believe about the God of Scripture. First, He exists. Second, He reigns supreme: He is omnipotent (all-powerful), omniscient (all-knowing), and omnipresent (always present everywhere). Third, He is loving, and kind, and gracious, and caring, and honest.

We can trust these above mentioned characteristics of God because they are expressed in Scripture. We believe them, even though we have never seen God: this is faith. Still, such faith is not a blind trust with a pie-in-the-sky mentality. If we believed every religious doctrine of the world, we'd be a mental mess of religiosity. But the Bible is our sole book for establishing our faith. If our faith is in ideologies apart from Scripture, we can be entrapped by every charismatic charlatan that comes down the pike. Our faith in God must be based on information gleaned from studying the Scripture. And because of events of Scripture, we believe God can multiply five loaves of bread and two fish into enough food to feed five thousand hungry men—even though we have never literally seen this happen.

If our watch is broken, we may not know what time it is, but time has not stopped, only our watch has stopped. Such is faith. And such was the case with the Apostle Paul. He never knew from day to day what difficult circumstances he would encounter, so, he expressed how he approached each day: "For we walk by faith, not by sight" (2 Corinthians 5:7). We may not be able to see what God is doing, but He is still working for us; therefore, our confidence in God should not

You Matter

diminish because we don't see Him at work.

I have never gotten my unique, glass clock to work, but time has not stopped working; rather, only my clock has stopped. Likewise, most of the time we can't see God work, and we don't necessarily know what He is doing, but that doesn't mean He has stopped working. So, we should live as if we can see Him working: this is faith.

Often, the problem with our faith is that we look at circumstances as we look at the clock: as if the clock is time, or that the clock regulates time, or the clock controls time. How ridiculous to allow a broken or imperfect clock to manage our activities, our emotions, and our plans, for time is external from the clock. And if all the clocks in the world stopped working, time would continue on course. So, I need to look at something more significant than my clock. Instead of looking at a broken clock and wondering if it's time to get up, how about looking at the sun? It still rises and sets. Or the seasons, for they continue. And the years keep coming and going, for we can tell that by our graying hair, wrinkles, and frequent aches and pains. Time is still moving on; therefore, we're getting older: in spite of our denial of birthdays.

Faith says, though we may not see God working, nor can we tell what He is doing, we know He exists, and He is working all things for our good! How can we know this if we can't see the evidence? We look at something more significant than ourselves, like the creation itself: it's still working. "The heavens declare the glory of God; and the firmament sheweth his handywork" (Psalms 19:1). But if Heaven and earth should be dissolved, we still have something more significant to look to: we look to His everlasting Word! "Heaven and earth shall pass away, but my words shall not pass away" (Matthew 24:35). All of us are in this picture. And God's Word has a lot to say about how He feels about us:

- He loves us (John 3:16).
- He is working all things for our good (Romans 8:28).
- He will never leave us nor forsake us (Hebrews 13:5).
- Christ ascended into heaven, but He promised He will not leave us comfortless (John 14:18).
- He will return someday to receive us unto Himself (John 14:3).

We sometimes view our lives as being inconsequential. We question: How can one life make a difference? How can I be a positive influence at my workplace? How can I affect my community? In time and space, we sometimes feel less than a flyspeck on a barn door. Such insignificance was somewhat the attitude among the disciples: "What is a child's lunch among five thousand hungry adults?" Faith responds differently. As a single spark can start a raging wildfire, faith the size of a small seed can change the landscape.

> And Jesus said unto them, Because of your unbelief: for verily I say unto you, If ye have faith as a grain of mustard seed, ye shall say unto this mountain, Remove hence to yonder place; and it shall remove; and nothing shall be impossible unto you.
>
> Matthew 17:20

You Matter

Christ created the universe, but he used a willing lad to share his lunch, and willing hands to dispense it, in order to feed the hungry multitude. Christ was the great denominator, but others played a role. He chose this process. That's why we matter to Christ.

Faith is not about our ability; it is about the size of our God! It is about our situation passing through His hands. Jesus blessed and broke and handed the bread and fish to the disciples. The lad's mother lovingly packed just enough lunch for her son that day, but that lad's lunch fed a multitude: with leftovers for another day. How? It passed through God's hands. When something comes from God, it comes from an endless source. God is the supplier; we are merely the distributors of what He places into our hands. Our lives, given into the hand of God, matter more than we can imagine!

You say, "I don't have much faith, so I am inconsequential in the kingdom." Such a statement is not true. A little bit of faith in our great big God can move mountains a thousand miles away. A young David defeated a giant and routed an entire army. An elderly Daniel took a solitary stand that effected an empire. One lowly maiden surrendered her body to the Creator, and nine months later, she gave birth to a baby who saved the world.

We question: How can my puny prayers make a difference? We argue: My paltry praise is too self-conscious to count. We sadly acknowledge: My small offering can't make a difference in a million-dollar church budget. We assume: My witness will be drowned out among the multitudes of vying voices. All are wrong! Still, that's where the disciples had pitched their tents. "What is this lad's lunch among so many?" they reasoned. We, too, falter on the turbulent seas of uncertainty. What significance is my limited talent among a field of professionals? Don't underestimate yourself, for God has chosen you for His work. Let me offer this illustration.

> We all enjoy beautiful music. The other day I listened to a rendition of Psalm 23.[1] This modern arrangement of these ancient words came alive to me like never before. An orchestrated arrangement touched the emotional cords of my soul. A soloist mesmerized me with his melodious voice; further, an accompanying voice harmonized during portions of the song, making me want to sing along. An almost two hundred and fifty voice choir joined in on the chorus, creating a thunderous crescendo that soared my spirit into the presence of the God Whom David wrote about.
>
> I've read this psalm a hundred plus times, and as a lad I had taken it to memory, but it never moved me like it did this time. My point? It has always been observed from a singular talent: the talent of the psalmist David. Yet, not meaning to minimize the talent of the shepherd of Israel, his singular talent has never moved me like this song did. So, we can see that an individual talent may have minimal impact, but joined with the talents of others, our role, no matter how minimal, adds to the totality of the potential. And when God anoints, wow! You may not

You Matter

be the star performer, but your voice matters. What if all choir members dropped out because they lacked the talent of the soloist? There would be no choir.

I doubt the psalmist felt his song was a best seller. But he wrote it anyway. Still, as a caution to some, we should never "think too highly of ourselves" (Romans 12:3). But our amateur abilities must not stop us from giving our best to the master. The value of my participation is not predicated upon my ability: it is my willingness to be available to Christ. Mind you, some shouldn't be in the choir, but there is a role for them somewhere in God's Kingdom. A nail in my hand is worthless, even dangerous, for I am not gifted as a carpenter. But a couple nails in the hands of Christ won redemption for all mankind. The difference in my insignificant ability being worthwhile or worthless is my willingness to offer it to the pool of talents that are present in Christ's Kingdom. That ability may simply be handing out bottles of water to choir members, but oh the praise that ascends to heaven from a choir of voices that are not dry of thirst. Let's not forget the adage: "For want of a nail ... ." You, too, matter.

The voice of the One Who spoke the universe into existence blesses your ability. This One does not simply exist in the universe; rather, the universe exists in Him. He is simply asking to borrow your sack-lunch. The one Who holds the small loaf of bread in His hands is ready to break and distribute it to the multitude, and He wants to do so through your hands. Your piddly sack-lunch, eaten alone, will pacify your growling stomach for a few hours, but offered up to Christ, can feed the masses. Passed through the hands of the One Who made the ten-thousand taste buds in each person's mouth, a loaf of bread can delight five thousand people with a single miracle.

Are you feeling insignificant in Christ's Kingdom? You're not the first. Moses did. He thought his advanced age and failing speech rendered him meaningless, but God wasn't finished with his life. Though he reluctantly accepted the challenge, with a shepherd's staff he rescued a nation from slavery, and he wrecked with a rod the empire that lorded over them. As God was not finished with the washed up and banished Moses, neither is God finished with you. Simply surrender yourself to the One Who needs a server to distribute the miracle loaves.

If you've read the inspiring biography of Gladys Aylward's life as a missionary to China, you may recall her sitting at the edge of the Yellow River, forlorn and hopeless. This was during the Sino-Japanese War, and after rescuing a host of orphaned Chinese children from the invading Japanese army, this tiny lady could not get them across the mile wide river, because there were no available boats. After four days of waiting, they ran completely out of food. One of the children realized Gladys' despair, and in an attempt to encourage her, reminisced about the Bible story of Moses and the Red Sea crossing. Whereupon Gladys exclaimed, "I am not Moses." To which the young girl countered, "But God is still God." Shortly after this conversation, an unexpected source of rescue came along.

You Matter

Gladys, along with all one hundred children, eventually made it to safety.[2] "Except we become like as children ..." someone once said, there's no place for us in Christ's Kingdom.

Your talent, or lack thereof, is not the issue. What is on trial is your willingness to give yourself into Christ's service. You are called into the service of the Great "I Am" of Scripture. That, dear one, makes all the difference. You matter to God! And when you submit to God, nothing else matters.

Endnotes
1) Shane and Shane album, Psalms Volume 2, Surely Goodness, Surely Mercy, 2015, Sung by Brooklyn Tabernacle Choir, 2018
2) The Little Woman, Alan Burgess, Buccaneer Books, Cutchogue, NY, 1959

A Mistake To Avoid

Mistaken Point is a literal place located on the southeastern coast of Newfoundland. Many a ship has been destroyed in the typically foggy weather of the region because sailors sometimes assumed they had reached Cape Race, and so, according to the charts, they should turn north. Wrong! For in turning north, they sailed immediately onto treacherous rocks. As regarding the name, the tale goes that when one particular ship captain wrongly assumed this point was Cape Race and turned his ship north, as he peered through the dense fog and suddenly saw rocks projecting out of the water, he proclaimed to the officers on deck, "Well, that was a mistake." And so, the locals appropriately called the area Mistaken Point.

There is another interesting occurrence at Mistaken Point. In this area, over time, the receding water and crashing waves exposed abundant layers of fossils that were discovered in the latter 1900s. These types of fossils are rarely found elsewhere: here they are numerous. We, who believe in God, marvel at His creation, intrigued by the minute details. But those who don't believe in the God of Creation, and who believe in evolution (that all life happened by chance over millions of years), say that this discovery offers answers to deep mysteries of evolution.

These fossils of small centimeter-size critters are said by evolutionists to be between 580-560 million years old. They are assumed to be a giant leap from the three-billion-year period when they believe the evolutionary stage was dominated by microbes: organisms too small to be seen without a microscope. They say this is when life got big: when microscopic life evolved into tiny, squiggly creatures. They further claim that in the next stage of the evolutionary process, critters got bigger and more complex, and eventually animals evolved. Then, some four to eight million years ago, the lineage of humans split from the chimpanzee lineage, and over the last few million years, humans evolved. And they use the discovery at Mistaken Point to support their theory.

I want to go on record with the old sea captain who proclaimed, "Well, that was a mistake." Man did not evolve from the animal world. And quoting my high school psychology teacher, I offer this explanation: "Where there is a creation, there must be a creator."

Consider, if we simply evolved, we are all meaningless creatures on a meaningless journey with no purpose. Not so! We did not accidentally happen. We were purposefully created by an all-knowing God with a plan for humankind. He created us with a mind that can invent, and we have a memory that can store indefinitely and connect all the stored knowledge with purpose. Just look around you at what humankind has done. You say, "Computers can do that." No, computers can do only what the designer creates them to do. But we humans go beyond what we see: we have the ability to love, to feel emotion, to enjoy pleasure, to reason, and to create friendships. This didn't happen by chance. There is a master designer. There is

A Mistake To Avoid

a creator, an intelligent planner and sustainer of the entire universe: "In the beginning God created the heaven and the earth" (Genesis 1:1).

Evolutionists argue that creatures evolved from the sea and from the substance of the earth over millions of years, all by chance and circumstance. However, Moses, the writer of Genesis, wrote some 3,500 years before evolutionists ever formed their theories, that the creatures were formed from the sea and from the land at the spoken command of God. "And God said, Let the waters bring forth abundantly the moving creature that hath life, and fowl that may fly above the earth in the open firmament of heaven" (Genesis 1:20). "And God said, Let the earth bring forth the living creature after his kind, cattle, and creeping thing, and beast of the earth after his kind: and it was so" (Genesis 1:24). Could the writer of Genesis have been that lucky at guessing? Absolutely not! The God of creation revealed to Moses how He created all the living creatures of the earth: by His spoken command.

When the evolutionists tell the account of creation, because they leave God out, it takes billions of years. But when you put God into the equation, it takes a moment: the spoken word. "And God said, "Let there be light" (Genesis 1:3) … "Let the earth bring forth" (Genesis 1:11) … "Let the waters bring forth" (Genesis 1:20). In a moment God said let there be life … and it happened!

When you leave God out of the equation, it may take the doctor, or the lawyer, or the scientist, or the therapist, or the programmer, or the project manager a year, or two, or three. Put God into the equation, and it can happen in a moment! That's why there are a multitude of ex-addicts sitting on church pews, who kicked alcohol and drugs with one trip to the altar.

The assumption from the discovery at Mistaken Point is still a mistake: these critters did not evolve. God created them by design and His spoken Word. He first conceived it, then He spoke the creation into existence. However, with humankind, creation was uniquely special, for He formed man with His own hands, and in His own image, and with an eternal purpose! You and I are not an accident. We are the unique design of God, created by God, and loved by God. And though rebellious against God, He has made opportunity for us to know Him again as Adam and Eve knew Him in the garden.

If one can believe that for three billion years there existed nothing but microscopic organisms that accidentally came into existence, that the earth froze solid and these became extinct, then one has a really big imagination. Such an imagination is big enough to have faith in a Creator God.

If one can believe that when the earth thawed, there developed—by chance—a more advanced form of life (the squiggly critters in the ocean, whose fossils were discovered at Mistaken Point), and after millions of years of evolution, various chains of life formed, and from one of these millions of life-chains, animals developed, then one has enough faith to believe in a Heavenly Creator if one would turn aside from doubt and seek after God. If one can believe that a human chain broke away (and coincidentally, at the same

A Mistake To Avoid

time, and by chance, believe that plant life evolved to sustain all these creatures), then you can believe anything, because you have an ultra-giant imagination. So, with such an imagination, why not consider there is a God? A genius Creator who planned it all. The good news: this is true. And more good news: this God loves you. Further, He wants to reveal Himself to you. A promise of Scripture that has been realized by many says, "And ye shall seek me, and find me, when ye shall search for me with all your heart" (Jeremiah 29:13).

Mankind became convinced that he didn't want nor need the God of creation; instead, they created their own ideas for a god: a god whom they designed. Their gods lacked the loving qualities of the God of creation. This happened early on, and it led to where we are today: "Because that, when they knew God, they glorified him not as God, neither were thankful; but became vain in their imaginations, and their foolish heart was darkened" (Romans 1:21). And so, the gods they created demanded such atrocities as their children be sacrificed to appease the god's anger. Their gods became monsters in their minds and powerless to assist them in life's necessities. But the God of creation came and redeemed mankind from his folly. I'm speaking of Jesus and Calvary. The God of creation included redemption in His master plan: "... the Lamb slain from the foundation of the world" (Revelation 13:8). Before God created mankind—with the freedom to choose obedience to God's ways, or to choose sin which corrupts and destroys—He planned a means of redemption for His creation.

Those who disqualify this loving God of creation and deny

His existence, need an out for their rejection of God: evolution, a creation that happened by chance, with no master designer, creator, or controller. They have figured out much about life's substance, but they have ignored the source. And billions of years of evolving becomes their coverall. They're still trying to fill in the blanks from 6,000 year-old-finds to their proposed 50,000—1,000,000 year-old-finds. I don't buy it! There should be a perfect chain of bones, with no gaps—especially thousands and even millions of years in gaps. The truth? The six thousand year history of mankind's existence is recorded in Scripture. Mankind simple refuses to accept it: evolution has become his panacea—and his excuse for not serving the Creator.

I like having a clock in every room, so, I buy clocks. Consider this clock-search illustration for the absurdity of evolution. On one such day of clock hunting, if I show up at an evolutionist's clock shop, the conversation might go something like this:

"Is this Swiss made?" I ask.

"No, no, no. It's a very unique clock. No one made it. It evolved over millions of years," the evolutionist replies.

"Really?" I ask, surprised. "But it's exactly the time, hour, minute, and second as my time. Someone had to set it. Did you set the time?"

"Oh, no. It came into my shop already set. Over millions of years it just evolved to the right time."

A Mistake To Avoid

"But it says, "Made in China" on the bottom. Can you explain that?"

"I know it says that, but it was not made in China. Over millions of years of evolution, it coincidentally took on those letters, probably not China at first, but with millions of years of evolving it could say anything. It just happens to be in the "Made in China" era," he explains, somewhat surprised at my ignorance about how things change over millions of years.

I accidentally drop the clock, whereupon he becomes angry. Picking up the pieces, he says, "Look what you have done. A clock, millions of years old, is now worthless." He scolds me.

"Just put it in a box and place it on a shelf," I console him, "and in a million years it may put itself back together. Or better still, it might become a clock-maker."

A silly story, you say. Perhaps, so, I defer back to my high school teacher: "Where there is a creation, there must be a creator." We had better figure out who the creator is, and once we figure that out, we need to recognize Him as our God. The Bible tells us who the creator is: "For by him were all things created, that are in heaven, and that are in earth, visible and invisible, whether they be thrones, or dominions, or principalities, or powers: all things were created by him, and for him" (Colossians 1:16). This Scripture is referring to Jesus: Designer, Creator, Sustainer, and Savior.

Here are three reasons to believe in the Christian God of Creation:

1) It is the best odds:
> If the Bible is in error, and if in the end I find out it was unnecessary to live the Christian life, I can still say, "I've enjoyed the journey. It has brought me much joy and peace and hope." But if I reject the Bible and the God of Scripture, and in the end find out it is true, I will have eternity to regret the decision. How long is eternity? Someone tried to describe it in a way that our finite minds might have some comprehension: If once a year one of the birds (that lives on the sandstone surface of the front of the church I pastor) pecks at the stone until he gets one small grain of sand in its beak, and he flies away and does the same year after year, when he has completely taken away all the stone that covers the front of the building, eternity may have begun.

2) I've found the Scripture regarding salvation to be, and to do, exactly what it says:
- At repentance and baptism, my condemnation—condemnation because of my sins—left, and my heart experienced overwhelming peace.
- At my Holy Spirit baptism, I spoke in tongues as others did some 2,000 years ago at the initial baptism of the Spirit (Acts 2:1-4). Further, I experienced the joy unspeakable referenced in Scripture.

A Mistake To Avoid

- Fear of death is gone, replaced with daily hope: I look forward to heaven with great expectation.

3) God has answered many specific prayers:
- Battles I could not win, He won for me.
- Financial blessings have been abundant.
- I have experienced personal healing in my body.
- God gave me provision when I could not see an answer to my problem.

When all those who have rejected God and feel they don't have to answer to Him, stand before God on judgment-day, and God asks for an explanation of why, the most logical explanation they have will be similar to the ship captain at Mistaken Point: "Well, that was a mistake." As for my decision for Christ, after fifty-five years, I'm able to say, "That was the best decision I've made in all my life."

It's not difficult to become a Christian: it's a few steps process:
- Acknowledge God and your need of salvation (Hebrews 11:6).
- Confess your sins and ask forgiveness (I John 1:9).
- Submit to baptism into the name of the Savior: the Lord Jesus Christ (Acts 2:38).
- Experience God's promise to fill you with His Spirit (Acts 2:1-4, 39).
- Continue in your Christian walk: "But grow in grace, and in the knowledge of our Lord and Saviour Jesus Christ... ." (2 Peter 3:18).

Most religions are man chasing after the gods; Christianity is the singular God of the Bible pursuing man. And God went out of His way to rescue you. Wow! You must matter a lot to Him. Avoid the mistake of rejecting Him by creating your own gods: evolution, self-reliance, elusive dreams, temporary pleasures. Don't allow your eternal regrets to echo the sentiments of the errant, ship captains of yesteryear: "That was a mistake."

Life at best is tough. There are dangerous rocks ahead, with mistakes you need to avoid. And Christ knows the way, for He is the way, the only way to safe shores. But if you've taken the wrong course and feel your life is already shipwrecked, don't despair. The life-raft called grace is waiting for you to climb on board. And the rescue captain? Jesus Christ. He's extending a hand for you to join Him. There's no better time than right now. And such a decision is never a mistake!

Dealing With Our Sins

The greatest burden mankind has to bear is the guilt and shame of sin. Like a faulty DNA predetermining one will have a specific disease, unchecked sins run rampant. We don't have to learn how to sin, for like a crying baby, sin is innate. A baby cries because that's what babies do; a sinner sins because he's a sinner. Children are drawn to sin. Why? Because of a sinful nature: graduating into more serious sins over time. This is not to suggest that young children are judged and sent to hell. But we can't ignore the fact that even before the age of accountability, children are impacted by their sinful nature. In the process, guilt mounts. And guilt not dealt with properly effects adversely.

At a young age we slip into our default mode: an Adamic nature, prone to lie, cheat, and steal. As adults we commit behaviors that leave us overwhelmed with regret and shame. Such actions alter our lives in a negative manner. Long after our failures, we make decisions based upon a conscience plagued by past guilt, fear, and falsehood. This was the testimony of David. After he miserably failed God by committing adultery with Bathsheba, the wife of one of his close military officers, Uriah, he attempted to hide his sinful act by deception. He called Uriah from the battlefield in hopes that he would spend a night with his wife. The ruse did not work, for

Uriah was more honorable than David, and he refused to go home to his wife when his comrades were still on military assignment. With narrowed options, David orchestrated Uriah's death, in hopes that this would hide his sin. In time, the shame became buried in the business of running a kingdom. But hidden sin harms the soul and drains the spiritual life. And our sin is never hidden from God, but God is too merciful to abandon us to sin's deceit. Guilt is a gift from God to bring us to our senses.

After some time, God sent the prophet Nathan into David's throne room to remind him that there is a supreme throne to which all mankind must submit. Nathan's story of a wealthy man, who took a poor neighbor's pet lamb to feed his guest, inflamed David's passion for justice and mercy (2 Samuel 12). But not until Nathan pointed a finger and proclaimed, "Thou art the man" did David's conscience revive. David's anguish of soul is acknowledged in the Scripture:

> Have mercy upon me, O God, according to thy lovingkindness: according unto the multitude of thy tender mercies blot out my transgressions. Wash me throughly from mine iniquity, and cleanse me from my sin.
>
> Psalm 51:1-2

David's hope resided in God's law of mercy. Under the Jewish religion there was provision for dealing with sin by following the Mosaic Law: a particular ceremony designed to avert God's punishment for sin, called the Day of Atonement (Leviticus 16, 23).

Dealing With Our Sins

The ritual consisted of diverse actions taken against two goats; one was killed, while the other was released into the wilderness. The goat that was killed represented mankind's sins being compensated for by death. The released goat represented mankind's sins being far removed from him. This sacrificial ritual was good for a year only and had to be repeated each year. It was a time of solemnness, yet great rejoicing, for Israel's sins were taken away by a substitute sacrifice.

But David felt no relief from such substitutionary death. Why did he not simply accept the substitute sacrifice designed by the Lord? He could have personally presented a sin offering to the priests. Perhaps it was because there were two sins which were not covered by the annual ritual nor by personal sacrifices: adultery and murder. David had committed both. The only remedy under the Jewish religion for these two sins was capital punishment. Heretofore, the only reasons David had escaped punishment were that his sins remained secret to but a few, and as king, his army of seasoned and loyal soldiers would have defended him to the death. Who would dare tackle this issue? So, David temporarily escaped judgment.

Still, though he escaped the reprisal demanded by the Mosaic Law, he could not escape the guilt and shame caused by his sins. The symbolic sacrifices of the Jewish religion were insufficient and did not work for David. They left him remembering his sin. The ritual slaughter of the goat proved insufficient to pay his debt of sin, nor did the symbolic release of the other goat remove the anguish of memory: shame remained in his heart. These—memory and shame—like a recurring nightmare, remained before him.

Sin has far-reaching pain. Often, it creates a separation from God, family, and associates. Consider Ahitophel, one of David's closest advisers but also Bathsheba's grandfather. Disappointment, hurt, and anger at David drove him to align himself with David's rebellious son Absalom, who attempted to steal the kingdom and kill his own father. But this alignment ended in Ahitophel committing suicide.

Even forgiven sin leaves consequences. After David sought and received God's forgiveness, he reaped the results of his sin. Joab, David's general, though a family member, used David's failures to try and influence his decisions. Deceitfulness within David's kingdom never ceased.

Further, sin's guilt has a way of causing one to feel unworthy of the promises of Scripture. The sacrifices in the Old Testament (Exodus 29:38-46), though symbolic, were designed to do three things:
- To allow God to meet and speak with His people by erasing the separation line caused by sin. Note, when confronted by the religious leaders regarding an adulterous woman, Jesus expanded upon the law as he wrote in the sand. Likewise, our sins are easily erased by God's hand of mercy (John 8:3-6).
- To make holy the place of worship, the ministers who lead the worship, and the people who participate in worship. This qualifies us for God's holy presence:

Dealing With Our Sins

"Follow ... holiness, without which no man shall see the Lord" (Hebrews 12:14).
- To allow the sinless God of creation to remain the God of a people who still sinned. Unlike in the Garden of Eden, God did not cast them out of His presence; rather, He made provision for the atonement of their sins. Grace was introduced: a foreshadow of Calvary and Christ's proclamation: " ... Father, forgive them; for they know not what they do ..." (Luke 23:34).

Still, individuals struggle in accepting forgiveness, and many, if not most, because of guilt and shame, live way below their privileges with God. Though God has judged, found guilty, and accepted Christ's substitute payment for man's sinful acts, mankind tends to continue to judge himself harshly and wrongly.

Though David's sins mentally towered higher than the altar's sacrifice, and they lingered long after the fire of the sacrifice had died out, his knowledge of God as a loving shepherd caused him to seek God's mercy. Though his anguished soul lamented, "The sacrifices are not working for me," he discovered, "The Lord is nigh unto them that are of a broken heart; and saveth such as be of a contrite spirit" (Psalms 34:18). And he penned his regrets: "For I acknowledge my transgressions: and my sin *is* ever before me" (Psalms 51:3). In his quest for restoration with God, he realized something most others of the Old Covenant did not: the sacrifices only worked because Immanuel would come and personally pay mankind's debt of sin. From prophesies that David wrote, we can surmise that he glimpsed the coming Christ, the coming eternal sacrifice, the lamb of God that

John identified. Consider one of the psalms which David wrote, its message fulfilled in Christ's crucifixion:
- Psalm 22:1—Jesus' cry from the cross
- Psalm 22:7-8—What those passing by Calvary said to Jesus
- Psalm 22:14—Bones pulled out of their sockets, but no bones broken
- Psalm 22:15—The plea from the cross: "I thirst"
- Psalm 22:16—The crucifixion
- Psalm 22:18—Garments taken and gambled for

In the inaugural sermon of the church, the Apostle Peter referenced the prophecy of David (Acts 2:25-32).

> I have set the Lord always before me: because *he is* at my right hand, I shall not be moved. Therefore my heart is glad, and my glory rejoiceth: my flesh also shall rest in hope. For thou wilt not leave my soul in hell; neither wilt thou suffer thine Holy One to see corruption. Thou wilt shew me the path of life: in thy presence *is* fulness of joy; at thy right hand there are pleasures for evermore.
>
> Psalm 16:8-11

David had to make a decision: Shall I live with guilt? Or shall I live with forgiveness? What gave him the right to step beyond his guilt and shame? When he foresaw the crucified Lamb of God, he was able to realize forgiveness for his sins. In a seemingly hopeless situation, he found hope in Calvary's sacrifice. Likewise, we have

Dealing With Our Sins

one of two choices regarding our sins:
- We can live in our shame, seemingly powerless to stop sinning and continuing to acquire more guilt.
- We can accept the substitute sacrifice of the Lamb of God: Jesus Christ.

How do I accept Christ's sacrifice? Jesus gave the answer to this question to a very religious, sincere, and wise old man by the name of Nicodemus: "Jesus answered and said unto him, Verily, verily, I say unto thee, Except a man be born again, he cannot see the kingdom of God" (John 3:3). This puzzled Nicodemus. How can one be born again? "Jesus answered, Verily, verily, I say unto thee, Except a man be born of water and of the Spirit, he cannot enter into the kingdom of God" (John 3:5).

Two acts are included in this new birth message: born of the water (identifying with Christ's death through water baptism into the name of the Savior—Jesus Christ) and born of the Spirit (the infilling of the Holy Spirit). The Apostle Peter gave the same explanation to the guilty crowd at the birth of the church: "Then Peter said unto them, Repent, and be baptized every one of you in the name of Jesus Christ for the remission of sins, and ye shall receive the gift of the Holy Ghost" (Acts 2:38).

We, too, must follow this command of Christ and His apostles regarding the new birth. And in the process, we recognize that in His great grace, Jesus applied His sacrifice on Calvary to pay our debt of sin. And instead of being overwhelmed with guilt and shame for our sins, we are filled with appreciation, joy, and thanksgiving to the

Savior Who took care of our every sin at Calvary. This is by far the best way to deal with our sins.

Do You Want To Be Made Whole

And it came to pass, as he went to Jerusalem, that he passed through the midst of Samaria and Galilee. And as he entered into a certain village, there met him ten men that were lepers, which stood afar off: And they lifted up their voices, and said, Jesus, Master, have mercy on us. And when he saw them, he said unto them, Go shew yourselves unto the priests. And it came to pass, that, as they went, they were cleansed. And one of them, when he saw that he was healed, turned back, and with a loud voice glorified God, And fell down on his face at his feet, giving him thanks: and he was a Samaritan. And Jesus answering said, Were there not ten cleansed? but where are the nine? There are not found that returned to give glory to God, save this stranger. And he said unto him, Arise, go thy way: thy faith hath made thee whole.

Luke 17:11-19

There are multiple attitudes, habits, faults, and ideologies—ingrained within us from various sources—that are not Christlike. Not only are we sinners by default (it's our nature to sin), many sinful practices are generational: passed down by parents and cultures over the years as if they are okay, sometimes even expected: harmful habits, addictions, and prejudices. How do generational practices (whether harmful of not) get started? My family in the mountains of eastern Kentucky had some quirky ideas: one readily comes to mind. Never marry a redhead. Why? Who knows? Evidently, something negative happened somewhere along the way, and a clannish tradition developed that was passed on to future generations.

We justify carnal attitudes and actions, such as harboring a grudge, or hating a certain race, or holding at arms-length certain kinds of people. But the sin, or the carnal attitude and actions we fail to overcome or refuse to let go, will eventually come around to bite us. Example: A businessman participates in blatant gossip by his children against fellow siblings. This keeps the family in a state of upheaval. The businessman grows old, and to his surprise, one of his kids commands a coup against him. The children join forces and kick him out of the family business. He is devastated, but he shouldn't be, for his children simply did what he taught them was okay to do.

I share this example by permission from a friend:

> Her father was a grudger. He taught his family there were certain relatives you didn't speak to because of some situation of the past. She once got into trouble for talking to a relative at a family funeral: that relative was on the do-not-talk-to list. Such an infraction would upset him to the point that he would go for weeks without speaking to the family. When he did speak, it was often explosive and demanding.

Do You Want To Be Made Whole

His years of harsh parenting motivated her, at age twenty-one, to leave Ohio and move to Minnesota: seven hundred miles removed from her adversary. Ironically, her dad missed her so much that he sold everything and followed her to Minnesota. He assumed she would forget the past and live with them again, but she refused to do so. Now mind you, he loved her, but he just didn't know how to show his love.

She didn't have a car, so she rode the bus to and from work. But the bus stop was a long distance from where she lived. Her dad volunteered to pick her up and drive her to the bus stop. At the end of the day he picked her up at the bus stop and dropped her off where she lived. All the while that he did this, he never spoke to her. The interesting thing about this scenario is that both of them were confessing Christians.

Here's the problem: we're saved from our sinful past, but we allow our past to control us still, even torment us. We've been rescued from the bondage of sin, but we still allow our carnal nature to manipulate our actions. We've been redeemed by the Lamb of God, but we still listen to the accusing voice of our old master. We've been washed in the blood of the lamb, but we still allow the grime of our filthy past to identify who we are in the present. Thankfully, that can change. We need to realize that we're blood-bought, love-caught, emptied of our sins, and God-filled. Hey folks, even in our carnal state, we never really belonged to the devil, for he stole us from our heavenly Father's presence. He raised us as his own, but we were never his kin. We belong to God. We are the children of the King of kings. We were absent from his home for a while, but He searched for us until He found us. He rescued us from sins' captivity and wrapped His loving arms around us. He cleaned us up, and He took us back into His home. We are His creation, not the devil's. As born-again believers, we are God's children, and royal blood flows through our veins. We are heirs to everything He owns. We are not nobody. We are somebody. But a problem often remains as we act out the training of our past, a past when we were in captivity by the devil.

The question remains: How do I change? How do I let go? How do I realize who I am? How do I cast off these attributes of a carnal man? How do I forgive? How do I change my default mode from depression to happiness? From guilt to innocence? From fear to calm? From despair to hope? From sorrow to joy? Maybe you can't make it on your own, but you can through Christ, for the Scripture proclaims, "I can do all things through Christ which strengtheneth me" (Philippians 4:13).

Luke 17 records the account of Jesus encountering ten lepers. The Bible description states, they "stood afar off... ." This particular posturing is what their disease and circumstances had done to them. They cried out to Christ, "Have mercy," but Jesus didn't immediately heal them. Instead, He commanded them to go show themselves to the priest, for only the priest could pronounce them clean and allow them to reengage within society. In obedience—but perhaps with

Do You Want To Be Made Whole

a measure of doubt and disappointment—they started out to find a priest. While they were going, they realized Christ had healed them of their disease. With great delight, they sought out a priest who could reinstate them within society. All but one.

One returned and gave Christ praise. Whereupon Christ asked: "Were there not ten cleansed? But where are the nine? ... thy faith hath made thee whole" (Luke 17:17-19). Like the others, he was healed of the disease, but unlike the others, He returned to express his gratitude. And wow, did Jesus have another surprise for him! We don't know exact details, but it seems Christ took him into a higher realm than the others experienced. Christ made him completely whole, for wholeness is more than a healthy body; it includes mind and spirit.

Let me attempt to describe what may have happened. The others were healed of leprosy, but they were not made whole as this one man. Their skin was cleared of the oozing pulse of leprosy, but did their fingers and noses return? They could now stop at the corner grocery store, but did their emotional features remain scared? The priest removed the restrictions previously demanded on them, but did they continue to think like lepers? They could cast off the warning bells that hung around their necks, and they could stop crying out "unclean," but did they remain antisocial, unable to believe they were welcome in social circles? Did any of them find a wife, or return to a wife, because they still felt ugly and less of a man? Did they experience anxiety out of fear the disease would return? Were they able to develop friendships, or were they bitter that the disease had robbed them of friends? Did they remain angry at the priest who drove them from their community, or of neighbors who had abandoned them? Angry at a religion that had isolated them? They were completely healed of leprosy, but did they forever think and act like lepers? Did they bear emotional scars of their past, and were they dictated to by their prior shame? We're not certain about details, but we know that only one was made completely whole.

We can assume there remained with these men some former traits associated with their dreaded disease, all except the one that returned to Jesus to give thanks. He was made whole. Physically, mentally, emotionally, and spiritually. How? The same way you and I can be made whole; we do what we can, and God does the rest. Consider these steps the one leper took:

- He returned. He didn't receive his healing and run; he received his healing and returned to the healer. It's awesome to have our sins removed, but if we keep returning to Christ, He will fix a lot of other things. Too many times we come to the Lord only when we have a need, failing to realize that every time we come into the presence of the Lord, we are better for it.
- He worshiped. This was not a traditional recitation of thanksgiving; rather, he cried out "with a loud voice." There's something spiritually exhilarating about "crying out" to God. Why? Since God knows our thoughts, why do we need to cry out? Perhaps it's associated with God's worthiness, but I also believe it has to do with our personal transformation. We've got to cry out to God louder than the voices

Do You Want To Be Made Whole

screaming in our head telling us how bad we are. Our brain needs to hear what our heart knows: I am forgiven, I am able to overcome, I am able to let go, and I am able to forgive those who have wronged me. Say what you need and want to believe. Ever remind yourself: I'm no longer a leper!

- He fell face forward before the Lord. This expresses deep humility toward God and is an expression of gratitude. We're never too good not to need to bow at His feet. In our best state, let us remember the aged expression of an uncertain source but definitely by a grateful heart, "There go I but for the grace of God." Paul expressed, "And such were some of you: but ye are washed, but ye are sanctified, but ye are justified in the name of the Lord Jesus, and by the Spirit of our God" (1 Corinthians 6:11). I once was a leper, but now I am not. All because of you!
- He submitted to Christ. He put Christ's agenda first. He had parents, children, or an old job that he could have gone to first; instead, he put God first. If some received healing today, they'd be off golfing next Sunday. Sadly, God can't trust some people with a blessing.
- He stepped across racial barriers. The scene was one where Jew and Samaritan, who traditionally hated each other, allowed a human need to supersede personal preference. The Scripture points out that this man was a Samaritan, and Jesus referred to him as a stranger, but it is obvious the man left as a friend.

Here's a good rule to follow to have God's favor: place your fellow man in higher regard than yourself. Treat each child as if he/she might someday become POTUS. Become color blind to all.

- He placed a relationship with Jesus Christ before his traditional religion. He was a Samaritan, so we aren't sure how he fared with Judaism, but he did not run to the Jewish priest or his religious tradition; he ran back to Christ. Our religious traditions can put God in a box. Our religious traditions may say one thing, but what does the Bible say? Our religious traditions may say baptism should be done this way, or not at all, but what does the Bible say? Consider that every convert in Scripture was baptized in water, and Christian baptism in Scripture called the name of the Lord Jesus Christ at baptism. Many traditions abandon this new birth experience; however, relationship with Christ demands the new birth. When believers in the Bible received the Holy Spirit, they spoke in tongues, a language they had not learned. When God moved in, there was no pious, quiet, calm, and controlled worship; it was loud, from the heart, with exuberance: leaping, shouting, and loud exclamation. Yes, that's sometimes humbling, but it's also an expression of gratitude. It's one of the first steps to being made whole.

And so, some twenty years after those silent, awkward rides with her dad, my wife desired of the Lord a closer walk, and in so

Do You Want To Be Made Whole

doing she prayed, "Is there anything between you and me, Lord?" The Lord graciously gave her a vision, clear and simple: a heap of trash. She knew. She had not forgiven her dad. A trash heap twenty years old and seven hundred miles removed? Yep! Not only had it kept a distance between her and her dad all those years, but what other negative side effects did it harbor? It was time for her to be made whole.

To some degree, we are all incomplete. We need to be made whole. How does it start? Sincere desire. How do I express such? By bowing at Jesus' feet in humble gratitude for Calvary. And here's some more good news! It doesn't have to take twenty years to be made whole: Jesus made the Samaritan whole in a single moment. Allow God to speak a word of wholeness into your life. Today!

Forgiveness

Hate and violence abounds. Discord continues to tear our world, our nation, and our lives apart. Hardly a week passes that we don't experience the pain and sorrow of failed marriages, or families disintegrating, and friends parting ways out of disappointments and disagreements. Just because we are in the church does not eliminate us from hurts and wounds and bad judgments.

The bottom line is simply this: we can't get everyone to agree on everything. Interview two people who are in disagreement, and when you hear the story of one, you will say, "I understand. I see where you're coming from." Then listen to the other and you are inclined to say, "I understand. I see where you're coming from, also." Everyone sees things from their personal perspective, and they stand upon their perception.

Perceptions create complications. Few remedies pacify all. The solutions often expand the divide. The world's "war to end all wars" was but a pause button for countries to realign themselves against each other. As a nation we are so divided that it is doubtful we can ever be a United States of America. Churches have had feuds going on so long that there seems little hope that harmony within the pews can happen. Couples have gotten themselves into such complicated situations that there seems no way out other than divorce. Parents and children have been driven so far apart by misunderstandings and hurtful words and insensitivities that there seems no hope of ever being a family again. Friends have grown so distant that it seems there is no way to bridge the gap. Just yesterday I heard of a son who texted his mother and threatened that he would never visit her again unless she severed all relationships with a certain person from his past.

But there is hope for our society, and there is a way to cease all strifes. The Bible gives a solution for every hurt, every misunderstanding, every government dilemma, every family fight, every argument that has brought division, every disappointment, and every hate-filled act. It is an act so few are willing to do, but it works every time. The answer to society's ills is a biblical principle called forgiveness. Yet, the word itself often evokes arguments over who is to forgive whom. Still, when applied, it always works.

There are two parts to the subject of forgiveness: The first has to do with God: "For God so loved the world …" (John 3:16) that He made a plan for redemption. That plan was a means whereby He could forgive all our iniquities. Nothing else had worked. Throughout four thousand years of the Old Testament, God waited long for man to get relationships right, but they did not. Consider the mentality that existed in the Old Testament.

- Cain became jealous of his brother, but instead of working out the differences, in a fit of anger, he murdered Abel.
- God gave His covenant nation, Israel, a list of rules to

Forgiveness

live by, with stiff consequences and a forced form of repentance. It was designed to deter sin; instead, man sank into hypocrisy and used the details of the Law as an excuse for vengeance without guilt.

- David committed adultery with Bathsheba, the wife of one of his elite soldiers and the granddaughter of one of his closest advisers, Ahithophel. Though an atrocious sin, instead of seeking forgiveness, he took the road of deception, manipulation, selfishness, and murder. The unresolved issue escalated even further. Out of anger, Ahithophel sought opportunity to destroy David, but the plot failed. Ahithophel committed suicide out of disappointment and perhaps fear that David had escaped death. And though David sought and received God's mercy, continual turmoil plagued his family until the day he died and after.

As for taking the higher road of forgiveness, Joseph became the exception and our example in the Old Testament. There is no biblical mention that he blamed his brothers for his plight, though they were responsible for selling him into slavery, feigned his death, and lied to his father. Once Joseph acquired his ruling status in Egypt, he could have brought vengeance upon his brothers, but he forgave them instead. The result? Israel found provision and safety in Egypt, Joseph's family reunited, and his children experienced the joy and blessing of a relationship with their grandfather, Jacob. And there is no mention that Joseph sought revenge against the woman who lied about him and the master who sent him to prison for a crime he didn't commit. That's thirteen years of his life stolen: three as a slave in Potiphar's house and ten in prison.

Once their father Jacob died, Joseph's brothers assumed he would wreck havoc upon them. To their surprise, not only did he not get even, he elevated their lifestyle in the land Egypt. Consider the dialog between Joseph and his brothers:

> And when Joseph's brethren saw that their father was dead, they said, Joseph will peradventure hate us, and will certainly requite us all the evil which we did unto him. And they sent a messenger unto Joseph, saying, Thy father did command before he died, saying, So shall ye say unto Joseph, Forgive, I pray thee now, the trespass of thy brethren, and their sin; for they did unto thee evil: and now, we pray thee, forgive the trespass of the servants of the God of thy father. And Joseph wept when they spake unto him. And his brethren also went and fell down before his face; and they said, Behold, we be thy servants. And Joseph said unto them, Fear not: for am I in the place of God? But as for you, ye thought evil against me; but God meant it unto good, to bring to pass, as it is this day, to save much people alive. Now therefore fear ye not: I will nourish you, and your little ones. And he comforted them, and spake kindly unto them.
>
> Genesis 50:15-21

Joseph was the exception in the Old Testament, but the Josephs

Forgiveness

were few and far between. Mankind in general was slow to catch on to the blessedness of forgiveness; instead, he overrated the "eye for an eye" mentality. So, God said something like, "I've got to go down among them and teach them the blessedness of forgiveness." And so, God, the Creator of mankind, became a man. The author of the Ten Commandments took the podium and explained the spirit of the commandments. And he taught not by words alone; rather, he taught by word and deed.

- In one such example, men brought an adulterous woman to Jesus, demanding judgment. "He who is without sin, let him cast the first stone," Jesus responded. The God Who once wrote with flaming pen upon permanent tablets of stone "Thou shalt not commit adultery," stooped and wrote in shifting sand, leaving room for the story to be altered. This lesson forced her accusers to spare her life, but this act of Christ did not necessarily cause them to forgive her, nor did it produce repentance in their hearts, something that desperately needed to happen. They needed additional training in forgiveness, and so, on to Calvary and a message to a repentant thief. Not only do I forgive you, but "This day shalt thou be with me in paradise" (Luke 23:43). Did the thief earn forgiveness? Did he deserve forgiveness? It doesn't matter. Forgiveness isn't deserved or earned by you and me; it's given. How can that be? Christ earned it for us, and He dispenses it freely to those who ask.
- No matter how good mankind lives, he is a sinner by nature. So, Christ created a means whereby man can

have all his sins forgiven, and he can have the power to live above the sinful deeds of his fallen nature. Man can be born again, a spiritual birth that gives grace to subdue—not eradicate—the human nature. In order for this to happen, mankind needs a means of transformation. Christ went to the cross to fulfill this need. And hanging on the cross, the guiltless Savior, our sinless Lord, suffering at the hands of liars, murderers, thieves, and religious hypocrites, uttered words of hope. Forgiveness is available. Two truths made this possible. One, Christ, being sinless, allowed His sacrifice to apply to the debt of sin owed by mankind. The second, being God, He possessed the authority to do so. Thus, he made a life-changing proclamation when He spoke these words, "… Father, forgive them; for they know not what they do…" (Matthew 23:34).

When Christ uttered those words of forgiveness, the veil of separation in the temple split apart, opening a way for mankind to enter into God's presence. Hell lost its power, for a perfect sacrifice for sin prevailed. Death lost its grip, for Christ resurrected from the dead, setting in motion eternal life for believers. The doors to heaven opened wide for all, for Christ died for all: not for a select race, specific color, or one of pedigree. Sinful mankind once again had access to God. At Calvary, God did the only thing that would work for us: He forgave us! So, the first part of forgiveness is God's goodness and means to forgive our sins. Our part is acceptance and participation in His plan to remit sins. It's called the new birth.

Forgiveness

The second part of forgiveness is directed to those who have received Christ's forgiveness: it is the necessity of forgiving one another. Since we struggle in this area, Christ established a motivational principle: If we don't forgive, God won't forgive us (Matthew 6:14-15).

We are quick to respond, "They don't deserve my forgiveness." But the question remains: "No matter what someone has done to us, is our refusal to forgive them worth facing God with blame in our hearts toward someone?"

Some challenge, God is unfair with this rule. My enemy doesn't deserve to be forgiven. There should be an exception to the rule. Why should one be forgiven who will not apologize, will not change, will not admit offense, or will not ask for forgiveness? God has a principle for these challenges, but it doesn't cancel our necessity to forgive them anyway. We need to realize that forgiveness is not so much for the offender as it is for the one who has been offended. Somewhat like a medicine, lots of people are involved in the process of its existence, with the pharmaceuticals and stock-holders being a major benefactor, but the medicine works the most for the person taking it. And like taking medicine, when we forgive, this facilitates personal healing, no matter what the person who is the offender does. And medicine doesn't necessarily taste good, but it does the job. However, in many cases, forgiveness effects the offender in a positive manner, sometimes motivating him to repent and change. The Apostle Paul explained:

> Dearly beloved, avenge not yourselves, but rather give

place unto wrath: for it is written, Vengeance is mine; I will repay, saith the Lord. Therefore if thine enemy hunger, feed him; if he thirst, give him drink: for in so doing thou shalt heap coals of fire on his head. Be not overcome of evil, but overcome evil with good.

Romans 12:19-21

There are three important points regarding forgiveness that helps us, especially regarding deep offenses, to forgive individuals:

- Forgiveness does not mean the offense was okay. The offender was wrong in doing such. To forgive does not give the offender the right to do such to you again. You merely release them into God's authority. Vengeance belongs to God alone.
- Forgiveness doesn't come naturally. It's not our default mode, and it's incompatible with our carnal nature. You have to practice forgiveness. "… train yourself to be godly" (1 Timothy 4:7), Paul wrote. Just like the athlete preparing to compete in a contest, forgiveness takes much effort.
- Forgiveness is unconditional; it is not merited. Regarding forgiveness, Jesus told Peter, "I say not unto thee, Until seven times; but, Until seventy times seven" (Matthew 18.22). We don't decide who and when and how often we forgive. We simply follow Christ's directive and let go of every offense.

Here's the reality of life:
- Injustices will happen to all: Joseph, Daniel, Christ,

Forgiveness

you, and me. We can keep score and lose in the end; we can let go and trust God's perfect judgment for all circumstances.

- Holding onto bitterness and hurts will harm us spiritually, emotionally, and physically. Revenge becomes our master; releasing such allows freedom. Ahithophel, who refused to forgive David, became a suicide statistic. David, who wronged Ahithophel, became a statistic of the redeemed. And what about all the wrongs done to Joseph? In contrast to Ahithophel, Joseph forgave. It's no secret that he became second in command in the most powerful nation of the land. Forgiving others of their wrongs against us removes the shackles of revenge that bind us; it frees God's hand to elevate us.
- By refusing to forgive, we become somewhat like the one we refuse to forgive: not necessarily the same fault, but in a similar manner. Anger controls us, and revenge drives us. Both are sin, and both lead to poor choices. And neither are allowed into the Heavenly Kingdom.

Jesus told a parable ((Matthew 18:23-35) about a king and his servant who owed him millions of dollars, yet the king forgave the servant all his debt. The forgiven servant, in turn, sought out one who owed him a few thousands dollars and had him committed to prison. When the king heard of the actions of the one he had forgiven so very much, he became wroth, and he summoned the servant and retroactively reinstated his debt, making him liable once again for a debt he could never pay. Kings can do things like that. The question arises: When we refuse to forgive someone who trespasses against us, does God retroactively recall all our past sins? Something to ponder.

These two concepts regarding forgiveness can change the entire picture in the life of the offended and the offender. Forgiveness erases the animosity that exists; further, it reverses many wrongs, putting back together broken marriages, splintered families, and abandoned friendships.

These two principles make all the difference for us: God's faithfulness to forgive us; our obedience to forgive others. I've experienced both. Forgiveness works. Every time! In fact, it's the only thing that worked for me. I wholeheartedly encourage you to experience it.

Mercy Is Not Approval

Consider the dialog between Samson and Delilah just before he realized his strength was gone.

> And she said unto him, How canst thou say, I love thee, when thine heart is not with me? thou hast mocked me these three times, and hast not told me wherein thy great strength lieth. And it came to pass, when she pressed him daily with her words, and urged him, so that his soul was vexed unto death; That he told her all his heart, and said unto her, There hath not come a razor upon mine head; for I have been a Nazarite unto God from my mother's womb: if I be shaven, then my strength will go from me, and I shall become weak, and be like any other man. And when Delilah saw that he had told her all his heart, she sent and called for the lords of the Philistines, saying, Come up this once, for he hath shewed me all his heart. Then the lords of the Philistines came up unto her, and brought money in their hand. And

she made him sleep upon her knees; and she called for a man, and she caused him to shave off the seven locks of his head; and she began to afflict him, and his strength went from him. And she said, The Philistines be upon thee, Samson. And he awoke out of his sleep, and said, I will go out as at other times before, and shake myself. And he wist not that the Lord was departed from him. But the Philistines took him, and put out his eyes, and brought him down to Gaza, and bound him with fetters of brass; and he did grind in the prison house.

Judges 16:15-21

Prior to this sad event, there were no prison bars that could hold Samson; after this, he became helpless as a kitten in a snake den and was led about by a small lad. Samson's mistake? For too long he interpreted God's mercy as God's approval.

Samson made several mistakes that led to this tragic event, but during the mistakes, mercy remained his companion. He misinterpreted his prevailing strength as God being pleased with his sinful performance. Consider this series of decisions that led to God's departure from him:

- Contrary to the law of his God, he determined to marry a woman of the Philistines. Though his parents begged him to reconsider, he would not relent. On one of his visits to his girlfriend's community, a lion attacked him along the way. Through his miraculous strength, he killed the lion with his bare hands. He

Mercy Is Not Approval

assumed God's anointing was God's approval of his disobedience to parents and God's law.
- The marriage became a disaster, but since God used the occasion to get revenge upon the Philistines for their sinful ways—by burning their fields and defeating them in battle—it seemed to Samson that he and God had a good thing going. Once again, Samson interpreted God's mercy as God's approval.
- He befriended a harlot. The men of the community locked the gates to the town and planned to capture him in the morning before he left the brothel. Samson foiled their plan when he arose at midnight, and finding the gate locked, lifted it—including the posts that held it—and carried the gate on his shoulders and fled the city. Once again, Samson confused God's mercy with God's approval.
- Samson's life continued to spiral out of control when he fell in love with Delilah. His enemies conspired with her to find out the secret of his supernatural strength. Over time, she wore down his resolve, and he told her the secret. She heralded the men of the community, and they cut off his hair, but his uncut hair was but one factor in his Nazarite vow. His vow, not his uncut hair, was the source of his strength. However, Samson assumed he would do as before: use his brute strength and humiliate the enemies of God. But this time he found out that even God's mercy has its limitations. There is a point beyond which mercy does not go, and if we go beyond that

point, we go alone. That seems to be one of Samson's flaws: his aloneness with his decisions.

Many professing Christians misconstrue mercy:
- Because we feel His presence, and a touching song causes a tear to trickle down our cheeks, we assume God approves our lifestyle, even though it is out of harmony with His Word.
- The Christian community magnifies the message of God's love to the point that we assume there can't be an eternal hell. Surely a God of love wouldn't abandon us even though our lifestyles are contrary to Scripture. We assume His love overrides His rules; that His mercy supersedes His holiness. We hang our hats on mercy, and rightly so, for without mercy we are all hopelessly lost. But when we are honest about the Scripture, we know He is angry at the wicked every day; we also know His mercy is renewed every morning. But we fail to accept that His mercy is not approval of our decision to sin; conversely, our sins break the heart of God every day.
- Because of Christ's mercy at Calvary shown to the repentant thief, we assume it doesn't matter how we live, for love wins in the end. So, we rewrite the Word of God: there can't be an eternal hell, because that's contrary to a God of love; God dare not punish a person for choosing an alternate lifestyle if that's the persuasion into which they are more comfortable; there is no harm in same sex marriage if you are

Mercy Is Not Approval

committed to your partner; civil rights overrule biblical directives.

I would like to reaffirm from Scripture that there will be a final judgment of the righteous and unrighteous: that there is a literal, eternal place of punishment for sinners, for the backslider, and for those who interpret the Scripture to appease their chosen, sinful lifestyle. There is a point where even mercy cannot acquiesce to our sinful ways. There is an eternal place of punishment: " … the lake of fire" (Revelation 19:20; 20:10, 14-15), where mercy does not exist for God is not there.

Consider the multiple Scriptures that speak of eternal punishment:

> And they shall go forth, and look upon the carcases of the men that have transgressed against me: for their worm shall not die, neither shall their fire be quenched; and they shall be an abhorring unto all flesh.
>
> Isaiah 66:24

> So shall it be at the end of the world: the angels shall come forth, and sever the wicked from among the just, And shall cast them into the furnace of fire: there shall be wailing and gnashing of teeth.
>
> Matthew 13:49-50

> And cast ye the unprofitable servant into outer

darkness: there shall be weeping and gnashing of teeth. Then shall he say also unto them on the left hand, Depart from me, ye cursed, into everlasting fire, prepared for the devil and his angels:

Matthew 25:40-41

And if thy hand offend thee, cut it off: it is better for thee to enter into life maimed, than having two hands to go into hell, into the fire that never shall be quenched: Where their worm dieth not, and the fire is not quenched.

Mark 9:43-44

Many question: How is this going to happen? How can every human be judged? The cynics mock: This sounds like a fairy tale. But the Bible has proven itself true in changing sinners' hearts, so why would it be false about its teaching regarding the eternal punishment of the wicked:

First: The Bible teaches that though our physical bodies die, we are all "living souls" that must spend eternity somewhere. We will not simply vanish into nothingness as if we never existed. The world as we know it will be destroyed, but the eternal souls of mankind will live on forever, somewhere.

> But the heavens and the earth, which are now, by the same word are kept in store, reserved unto fire against the day of judgment and perdition of ungodly men. But the day of the Lord will come as a thief in

Mercy Is Not Approval

the night; in the which the heavens shall pass away with a great noise, and the elements shall melt with fervent heat, the earth also and the works that are therein shall be burned up. Seeing then that all these things shall be dissolved, what manner of persons ought ye to be in all holy conversation and godliness, Looking for and hasting unto the coming of the day of God, wherein the heavens being on fire shall be dissolved, and the elements shall melt with fervent heat?

1 Peter 3:7-12

Second: The Bible declares that Satan and his angels will be judged and punished eternally.

And the beast was taken, and with him the false prophet that wrought miracles before him, with which he deceived them that had received the mark of the beast, and them that worshipped his image. These both were cast alive into a lake of fire burning with brimstone.

Revelation 19:20

The Bible is even specific about certain individuals: the devil, the false prophet, and the rich man who showed no mercy to the poor:

And the devil that deceived them was cast into the lake of fire and brimstone, where the beast and the false prophet are, and shall be tormented day and night for ever and ever.

Revelation 20:10

And it came to pass, that the beggar died, and was carried by the angels into Abraham's bosom: the rich man also died, and was buried; And in hell he lift up his eyes, being in torments, and seeth Abraham afar off, and Lazarus in his bosom.

Luke 16:22-23

Third: Mankind will be judged and given an eternal appointment of either God's abode, or Satan's abode.

And the smoke of their torment ascendeth up for ever and ever: and they have no rest day nor night, who worship the beast and his image, and whosoever receiveth the mark of his name.

Revelation 14:11

We dare not pick and choose regarding what the Bible says about eternal damnation. There are too many Bible references to a final judgment for us to scoff:

And I saw a great white throne, and him that sat on it, from whose face the earth and the heaven fled away; and there was found no place for them. And I saw the dead, small and great, stand before God; and the books were opened: and another book was opened, which is the book of life: and the dead were judged

Mercy Is Not Approval

out of those things which were written in the books, according to their works. And the sea gave up the dead which were in it; and death and hell delivered up the dead which were in them: and they were judged every man according to their works. And death and hell were cast into the lake of fire. This is the second death. And whosoever was not found written in the book of life was cast into the lake of fire.

Revelation 20:11-15

Of course, there are those who laugh at the concept of eternal punishment, a lake of fire, or a sea of fire that doesn't burn out, and terms such as fire and brimstone. The Apostle Peter warned that scoffers would speak against a final judgment:

And saying, Where is the promise of his coming? for since the fathers fell asleep, all things continue as they were from the beginning of the creation. For this they willingly are ignorant of, that by the word of God the heavens were of old, and the earth standing out of the water and in the water: Whereby the world that then was, being overflowed with water, perished: But the heavens and the earth, which are now, by the same word are kept in store, reserved unto fire against the day of judgment and perdition of ungodly men. But, beloved, be not ignorant of this one thing, that one day is with the Lord as a thousand years, and a thousand years as one day. The Lord is not slack concerning his promise, as some men count slackness; but is longsuffering to us-ward, not willing that any should perish, but that all should come to repentance. But the day of the Lord will come as a thief in the night; in the which the heavens shall pass away with a great noise, and the elements shall melt with fervent heat, the earth also and the works that are therein shall be burned up. Seeing then that all these things shall be dissolved, what manner of persons ought ye to be in all holy conversation and godliness, Looking for and hasting unto the coming of the day of God, wherein the heavens being on fire shall be dissolved, and the elements shall melt with fervent heat?

2 Peter 3:4-12

The Apostle Peter warned that scoffers would speak against the Scripture and major events of punishment recorded in Scripture, denying that they ever happened. The apostle said they would be here in the last days, and we now know of some who deny the authority of Scripture:

- They laugh at the story of the flood as our example of destruction and the rainbow as a sign of promise.
- They reject Sodom and Gomorrah as a pattern of destruction by fire caused by God's hatred of sin and His responsibility as "judge of all the earth" (Genesis 18:25).
- They disavow the teaching of Christ which affirms an eternal judgment.
- They reject multiple Scriptures which declare there is a final judgment.

Mercy Is Not Approval

The terms of Scripture (lake of fire, or sea of fire that doesn't burn out; fire and brimstone; earth melting with fervent heat) were written long before we knew of similar existing realities. Scientists have discovered four red orange planets similar to the earth, but they are too close to their sun, so they are molten rock. At 3,990 degrees Fahrenheit, they have a lava ocean twenty-eight miles deep. The heat is so intense it vaporizes the liquid rock, turning it into rock gas, which forms clouds, then the gas condenses and rains back to the lava planet, not as drops of rain, but as red-hot rocks.

You say of such a place of punishment, "the heat would annihilate humans." That's true. But this happens after the resurrection, and we won't have fleshly, human bodies as we do now; rather, ours will be a changed body. Just as a man whose leg has been amputated can still feel the phantom pain of the past, or experiences an itch where no leg exists, those cast into eternal punishment will feel pain, hopelessness, and the sense of an awful separation from loved ones and friends. That is why there will be anguish described as "weeping, wailing, and gnashing of teeth" (Matthew 8:12; 13:42, 50; 22:13; 24:51; 25:30).

I can't tell you at what point mercy stops, but there is a point where mercy can go no farther. And like God dealing with the rebellious Israelites he delivered from Egyptian bondage, He proclaimed, You can go over into the land as I promised, but I'm not going with you (author paraphrased). The lake of fire is one place I know there is no mercy. Jesus spoke a parable of such:

    And in hell he lift up his eyes, being in torments, and

> seeth Abraham afar off, and Lazarus in his bosom. And he cried and said, Father Abraham, have mercy on me, and send Lazarus, that he may dip the tip of his finger in water, and cool my tongue; for I am tormented in this flame. But Abraham said, Son, remember that thou in thy lifetime receivedst thy good things, and likewise Lazarus evil things: but now he is comforted, and thou art tormented.
>
> Luke 16:23-25

If there is no mercy in the lake of fire, is there some point on earth where we, by our rejection of God's will, frustrate mercy into leaving? Sadly, the Scripture speaks of such a danger zone.

> And with all deceivableness of unrighteousness in them that perish; because they received not the love of the truth, that they might be saved. And for this cause God shall send them strong delusion, that they should believe a lie: That they all might be damned who believed not the truth, but had pleasure in unrighteousness"
>
> 2 Thessalonians 2:10-12

How do you know you haven't passed over into that realm of apostasy? If you still believe the Scripture regarding heaven, hell, sin, and redemption through Jesus, you haven't crossed that point of no return. But as a sinner, you are camping outside the safety zone.

There is in the world of physics the idea of absolute zero

Mercy Is Not Approval

temperature. When the temperature reaches regular zero it can continue to drop, but at minus 459.67 degrees Fahrenheit, the temperature cannot go any lower. It is at absolute zero: simply put, it is absent of any heat. It is the point where atomic and molecular motion ceases. Absolute zero. But more recently, scientists, by some form of lab trickery, have manipulated atoms into an arrangement that causes the temperature to cross over, to go beyond absolute zero.

I see God and His mercy in this scenario, pushing the mark for us regarding mercy beyond the absolute threshold. "But God, who is rich in mercy, for his great love wherewith he loved us, Even when we were dead in sins, hath quickened us together with Christ..." (Ephesians 2:4-5). It happened for Samson. He had gone beyond where mercy was comfortable going. His life had ended up a miserable failure because he interpreted God's mercy as God's approval of the lifestyle he lived. But mercy lingered close by; it kept in eyesight his prison of blindness, an ear attentive to his voice, waiting and hoping. And over time, it happened! "Howbeit the hair of his head began to grow again after he was shaven" (Judges 16:22). This signified a Samson of prayer. Of remorse. Of repentance. And Samson found mercy again! Though Samson momentarily tied mercy's hands as he lay on Delilah's knees, it trudged alongside him as he turned the gristmill, desiring to give him another chance. And mercy sprang into action when he dared pray again.

The world had approached the absolute zero mark in sin, a place where sin abounded, and mankind seemed hopelessly lost; it was a place where mercy's power had reached absolute zero and could go no farther. Impasse. But God, with a wonderful love plan, stretched forth His hands upon an old wooden cross. As He clinched two nails for six long and lonely hours, mercy went beyond our faults, and we were spared eternal condemnation for our sins. He who knew no sin became sin for us. And seeing Him hanging on the cross, mercy manipulated beyond the absolute zero point, and though no one deserved it, mercy did its work anyway. It was a God thing!

Here's some more good news! Mercy still abounds. Let's not allow our past failures to prevent mercy from doing its present work. But you say, "I'm not sure I can stop sinning, so I don't want to make God angrier than He already is by my trying and failing over and over." Hold on there; you're listening to a lying devil. He's manipulating you just as he did Adam and Eve. And just as he did Judas as he fiddled with a noose.

Here's what you need to do. Too many mentally put the cart before the horse in their spiritual journey: a tough way to travel—pushing all the way. It's always good for you to seek improvement in your life, but go ahead and receive God's mercy now. Then work on being an overcomer (and God will help you) after you've accepted mercy, for you can't really get good until you've gotten God in your life. God's mercy is not God's approval of our sins; rather, it is His plan for the removal of our sins and the beginning of a new lifestyle in Christ Jesus. Ask anyone who has ever failed God but found Him waiting with open arms at an altar of repentance. Ask Abraham the liar. Ask Rahab the harlot. Ask David the adulterer. Ask Jesus Christ. Why ask Christ? Because He's the One Who died to take away the sins of the world. Yours and mine included. Now that's mercy!

Inject A Little Madness

Hay que poner un poco de locura a veces en la cordura. These were the words spoken by Eusebio Leal, for many years the official historian of Havana, Cuba. Translated, it means, "Sometimes you need to inject a little madness into the sanity."[1]

In 1967, in revolutionary Havana, Cuba, Mr. Leal learned that a heavy truck had cracked open the asphalt in front of the governor's palace. Upon investigating, he discovered underneath the pavement a colonial-era street made of wooden bricks. Known only to exist in two other cities in Europe, wooden bricks were certainly a rare find in Cuba. Back in the 1800s, a visitor to Cuba had written that he saw such a street, but no one knew where the street existed. This was an extraordinary discovery, so when the government sent in a load of asphalt to cover up the cracked pavement, Mr. Leal laid down in front of the steamroller and refused to get up. Civil disobedience in communist Cuba was a dangerous act, but this time it worked. The rare discovery was protected. That's what prompted this statement by Mr. Leal, "You sometimes need to inject a little madness into the sanity."

A portion of this rare, wooden street is now available for others to see. It didn't stop there: the madness seemed to continue.

The Cuban government gave Mr. Leal one million dollars to help create—something unheard of for decades—free enterprise in old Havana. That investment brought in $119 million in one year for a net profit of $23 million (bad news for socialism). Without the madness injected into the mindset of communist Cuba, the advances the Cuban people have experienced the past few years may never have happened.

I'm thinking of examples in Scripture where individuals injected a little madness into the sane and a little insanity into the norm:
- A teenage lad going up against a bear and lion that attacked his father's sheep seemed mad at best. But things got even madder. I'm imagining trained and seasoned warriors watching from the hillside overlooking the battlefield, just biding their time, hoping against hope for the giant, Goliath, to go back home. But young David injected some madness into their sanity: "I'll fight him!" But how? With a sling and a stone? That's utter madness, but it worked!
- Two young men—young Jonathan and his armor-bearer— scaled a wall of rock and confronted an entire outpost of Philistines. They injected some lunacy into their sanity. In theological terms this is called faith, but in tactical terms this is called fanatical. But faith defies the normal and sometimes goes against rational. And without faith, it is impossible to please God (Hebrews 11:6), so, inject a little madness and see what God will do.
- All the others lined the street in a usual fashion and

Inject A Little Madness

observed the procession of Christ and his disciples; that is, all except Zacchaeus. He does something different than all the others. This chief tax collector, in his business attire and spit-shined sandals, scaled a tree in order to see over the crowd and get a glimpse of Jesus. He injected some madness into the sanity of the crowd, but he's the only one in the group that had Jesus go home with him that day.

- The lone and sickly widow—who pressed her way through the crowd, hoping that, if she could touch the hem of His garment, she would be healed—wasn't far from tipping the sanity scale. Others waited for Him to touch them, allowing Jesus to set the agenda, but she injected some madness into the sanity of the crowd and walked away the wiser.
- His friends carried him on a stretcher through the dusty streets. They finally caught up with the crowd blocking the entrance into the house where Jesus ministered. Many waited to get inside the house, in hopes of a miracle from Jesus. But these men injected some madness into the sanity of the crowd, climbed upon the rooftop, removed a portion of the roof, and lowered their friend into the room where Jesus sat.

"Sometimes you need to inject a little madness into the norm." Regular activity generally produces typical results; extraordinary results seldom come from mundane requests, though Christ did, on occasion, act strictly out of personal passion.

I'm also thinking of God's response to moments of madness and what He thinks about our actions as He looks down from heaven. What are His thoughts? "That's normal faith: a normal human response, nothing extraordinary about that." Is that how He feels about us?

But once in a while, our madness touches the heart of God. Years ago, the child of a newly converted couple concluded that I, as pastor, was the Jesus talked so much about in church. "Here comes Jesus," he would say to his parents when he saw me walking the isle. I stopped in the center aisle once and greeted him, at which point he pointed to a scratch on his face and asked, "See this booboo?" "Yes," I responded. "Make it go away," he demanded. Childlike insanity!

Except you become like children, you can't enter the kingdom, Jesus explained. Why? The Kingdom of God defies the norm: tongues of fire, gifts of the Spirit, the dead brought back to life, living by dying, getting by giving, turning the other cheek and being blessed for doing so. None of these meet the qualifications for sanity.

Jesus saw Paul and Silas sitting in that jail cell, their feet fastened in stocks, their countenance sad, their movements slow and deliberate, their backs still bleeding from the open wounds made by Roman whips. He turned his head from the pitiful sight, but then He heard an unusual sound for a prison cell. At first, it was but a faint hum, then barely above a whisper, so Jesus bent an ear toward earth and listened intently. "To be like Jesus, to be like Jesus, on earth I long to be like Him,"[2] the words flowed in rhythmic tones from their lips, somewhat in a minor pitch but with passion.

Inject A Little Madness

Perhaps even God is set aback. He calls his angels and points to the scene: "Hey, Gabriel, I didn't see that coming." They sang into the evening, and God put another galaxy on hold just to listen. "Oh, I want to see Him, look upon His face ... ." A prisoner cried out, "Hey guys, could you knock it off! I'm trying to sleep."

"Sometimes you need to inject a little madness into the sanity," Paul said, or at least that's how I interpret the Scripture: "... to live is Christ, and to die is gain" (Philippians 1:21). So, the singing continued. "Tis so sweet to trust in Jesus ... ."[3] "In the sweet by and by ... ."[4] "I see a crimson stream of blood ... ."[5] On and on into the night they sang. If it had been in a church building, or at a concert, or in a recording studio, it would have been reasonable. But it was in a jail cell, their feet in stocks, their backs raw and exposed to flies.

The clock struck midnight, but the singing didn't stop. And God couldn't hold back. We can only imagine as to the following chain of events. God waved an angel onward. A meteorite-like power pierced the sky, exploding into an earthquake that shook the prison, and the doors popped ajar. What an eventful night! And best of all? The jailer and his family got saved.

To get the miracle you need, you sometimes have to inject some madness into the sanity that maintains the norm. You may have to step out from the crowd, lay aside emotions that constrain, and cry out into the silence, believing God in spite of the circumstances. I can't guarantee God will do things the way you want, but I can guarantee He sees you now, He cares, and He is sometimes taken aback by the faith-filled actions of His creation.

Sanity says you have cancer, and you're going to die from it. You may, but then again ... . Sanity says your child has made some poor decisions that will destroy her, and there is nothing you can do about it, but who knows for sure there's no hope. Sanity says you have to accept your circumstances as they are, so stop fighting the inevitable. Sanity says you don't have the ability, the education, nor the resources to make your dream come true. Sanity says stop trying to paddle upstream, just let the current carry you downstream like everyone else.

You sometimes need to inject a little madness into the sanity, for if you don't, you'll never reach the potential to which God has called you. The altar is one of those places where madness defies the norm: where you stretch your faith and believe for the impossible. A trip to the altar places you in an extraordinary position: one that says "yes" to God's promises.

He was young, with most of life still ahead of him. And he was rich, capable of buying his way into most settings. He indicated that he wanted to be saved. And he already obeyed all the commandments—at least he thought so—which Jesus said were essential. What could hinder him? Still, one directive of Jesus caused him to turn away: "Sell all you have and give the money to the poor and come and follow me and you will not only be saved, you will have treasures in heaven." Madness! Insanity! I can be of more benefit to the kingdom by my wealth than letting it go, he reasoned. So, he rejected Christ's directive, climbed back onto his camel, and his caravan plodded away. He turned his sorrow-riddled face for one final glance at Christ: the last time he would see Christ's

Inject A Little Madness

face until the final judgment. What an opportunity he lost because he chose the sane—and seemingly safe—way!

Jesus shook His head and sadly expressed to His disciples, "It's easier for his camel to get through a needle's eye than for him to get into the kingdom." So, no one who's wealthy will ever make it, the disciples reasoned among themselves, for no camel could ever squeeze through such a tiny slot.

Whereupon, Christ elaborated, "... With men this is impossible; but with God all things are possible" (Matthew 19:26). How? God is quite inclined to respond to the madness of faith: be one rich or be one poor. If ever there was an act of seemingly utter madness, it was Christ making provision for our salvation: Calvary. A crown of thorns. Humiliation galore. Hands and feet nailed to a cross until He died? Yes, that was the madness that Christ chose. And He's still madly interested in saving whosoever will.

Endnotes
1) The Man Who Saved Havana, Article by Tony Perrottet, Photography by Néstor Martí, Smithsonian Magazine, May 2018
2) To Be Like Jesus, author unknown
3) 'Tis So Sweet to Trust in Jesus, by Louisa M. R. Stead
4) In the Sweet By and By, Sanford F. Bennett, 1868
5) I See A Crimson Stream of Blood, Bishop Garfield T. Haywood, 1920

Is There Not A Cause

And David said, What have I now done? Is there not a cause?

I Samuel 17:29

This Scripture has been used in sermons by most every preacher across the land. And the story behind it is fascinating. It's taught in every Sunday School class across the globe: young David going up against Goliath while Israel's seasoned army watched. And David's defense against his accusing brothers is classic: this is simply a cause worth fighting for. The message lives on in many a courageous behavior. Here's one such act of gallantry:

On September 8, 2009, Dakota Meyer, a twenty-one-year-old Marine Sargent, was one of thirteen American military trainers embedded with a unit of eighty Afghan soldiers headed for a routine meeting with local elders in a village. In route, about one hundred and fifty Taliban fighters ambushed them. This heavy enemy-fire immediately trapped four of the US soldiers at the front of the force.

Positioned in the back of the column when the ambush began, Meyer disobeyed orders to remain in place, and instead, used a Humvee to rush forward into the kill zone to try and rescue the four soldiers trapped at the head of their column. Throughout a six-hour battle, Meyer—though wounded himself—rescued thirty-six Afghan and American troops in four attempts to reach the four trapped comrades. On the fifth attempt, he and team members broke through to the front and moved on foot through a hail of gunfire only to find the four American soldiers were dead. Meyer then retrieved their remains and protected them from the debauchery of the enemy.

The question arises: Why would Sargent Meyer and his men risk their lives as they did? The answer: The lives of the four trapped soldiers represented a cause that defied fear and personal desire to live.

Sometimes the cause is greater than the commands to wait for support. Some causes are worth defying reasoning. Some causes are worth going against standard procedures and traditional protocol.

In the end, Marine Sargent Meyer's superiors thought so too. They awarded him the Medal of Honor, making him the first living Marine to receive the Medal of Honor for heroism in the US wars in Afghanistan and Iraq.

A few spiritual heroes stand out in Scripture: men and women who defied logic and set aside protocol and trampled on religious traditions to get the attention of our Lord. A select journey through the Book of Matthew reveals some of these:

- A leper, who defied the legal restrictions regarding this terrible disease. Instead of calling out "unclean" as the Mosaic Law commanded, to warn those around him to keep a distance, he broke through the crowd,

Is There Not A Cause

fell at the Lord's feet, and cried out for the Lord to make him clean. (Matthew 8:1-4)

- A centurion, who being a Gentile and knowing the traditions regarding Jews mingling with heathens, defied reason and proclaimed, "Though I'm unworthy for you to enter my house, just speak the word, and my servant will be healed." (Matthew 8:5-13)
- A woman, who was ceremoniously unclean and could not touch anyone less she defiled them, decided, "If I can but touch the hem of His garment, His power may flow into me, and I can be healed." She defied not only Jewish Law, but reason as well, for she had been sick for twelve years, and she had tried all the specialists of her day, and surely she had personally prayed for healing. Reason said she had exhausted all her resources—especially her money—and was not going to get well, but her faith fought against the odds. (Matthew 9:20-22)
- A man—whose daughter died—defied all logic, and though the mourners were already assembled to start the funeral, he sought out Christ, saying, "You can bring her back to life." (Matthew 9:23-26)
- Friends brought to Jesus one who was demon-possessed, blind, deaf, and unable to speak. You can imagine the confusion as his friends dragged along the dusty street this defiant, confused, and tormented man and laid him at the master's feet. The poor soul had no idea what was happening to him until, suddenly, he was released by the demons, and he was

able to see for the first time his family and friends. He heard them exclaiming their praise to Jesus for what He had just done. And then he, to the joy of those present, uttered his first words. (Matthew 9: 32-33)

- A Canaanite woman resisted prideful emotions and insulting comments from the Lord as she pleaded for Him to deliver her daughter from demonic possession. (Matthew 15:21-28)

And then there was young David going alone onto the battlefield against the giant, Goliath, with sling, five stones, and a cause.

God is still in the business of causes: the sick, the wounded, the broken. Many wonderful miracles have happened in our midst. We could stop pressing for more, be thankful for what we've received, and spend the next few years rehearsing the testimonies of what great things God has done. But there is more God wants to do! The Lord never runs out of miracles. We run out of time, energy, faith, and patience, and we generally quit way before the Lord finishes, and sometimes just before the discovery of the mother lode of treasure. And as long as there is a cause, we should look to Christ for an answer.

The Lord Jesus' ministry continued to produce one more miracle, one more surprise. After three days of intense ministry, with many miracles taking place, instead of sending the crowd away, our Lord called for the seven loaves and a few fish. He blessed and broke the bread, gave the pieces to his disciples, and they fed four thousand

Is There Not A Cause

men, plus women and children. (Matthew 15:29-39)

We can settle for the status quo, but we don't have to. We have a host of scriptural examples to propel us into greater depths and higher heights and continual miracles. Mediocrity never impresses the Lord, but several examples in Scripture of extraordinary acts of faith did impress Him. We've shared some cases of those who defied logic and tradition and protocol. The Lord didn't slink away from their unorthodoxy; instead, He answered their request!

Every day is another opportunity for someone to touch heaven with their faith in spite of their circumstances: to dispute the report of the doctor by defiant praise to God, to challenge the forecast of the economic guru by giving the last dollar to support missions, to inspire God Himself by leaving the comfort zone of conventionality and stepping into the muddy waters of the Jordan. These are acts of faith that cause heaven to turn its awestruck attention to a body of believers who tackle their giants with a stone, a sling, and a shout of triumph unto God. Why? A cause greater than anything else.

Surely there is such a cause among us! Can we identify with Marine Sargent Dakota Meyer as he defied reason to rescue his comrades? Should not the multitude of trapped and wounded souls, ensnared by the devil and headed into eternity without Christ, bring out the fight in us? Are not our lost loved ones worth any effort we may make to reach them with the saving grace of Christ? Like Abraham of old, who defied the odds of God's preconceived plan to destroy the twin cities, let the prevalence of impending judgment propel us into a face-to-face encounter with God, and let us plead for His mercy over our loved ones. Such boldness from Abraham didn't annoy God; instead, He marveled that a man could be so passionate about the lost. "And it came to pass, when God destroyed the cities of the plain, that God remembered Abraham, and sent Lot out of the midst of the overthrow ..." (Genesis 19:29). Wow! A man interceding with God for another human.

Abraham's plea to spare the cities came up short (for ten righteous could not be found), and judgment came. Still, many had the opportunity for salvation, and in the end, Lot and two daughters were spared. However, the debauchery that followed (Genesis 19:29-38) is despicable: a drunken Lot fathered sons of his own daughters. This was a carryover from the influence of the wickedness of Sodom upon Lot's family. The story didn't end with God's destruction of the twin cities and the incest that followed. God brought good out of the debacle. The Bible heroine, Ruth, a Moabite, born years later into the lineage of Lot's incest with his daughters, became a progenitor in the genealogy of Jesus Christ (Matthew 1:5-6, 16).

And the story doesn't stop because of the failures of one, or two. God's cause continued in the miracle birth of Christ. Messiah continued to a mount called Calvary, but His crucifixion there did not stop God's cause. From Christ's death, miraculously, a new lineage started: the lineage of the redeemed, made up of both Jew and Gentile. And many of us are in that family. Isaiah of old asked a question of us: "... and who shall declare his generation? for he was cut off... ." I'm so glad Abraham recognized there was a cause to intercede before God for his generation. Let's be sure we do the same for ours.

Memento Mori: Remember to Die

> For whosoever will save his life shall lose it: and whosoever will lose his life for my sake shall find it.
> Matthew 16:25

In ancient Rome, so says tradition, the emperor paraded conquering military generals— returning from the war—through the streets in an elaborate display of pageantry. This tradition honored the general by his peers and allowed the citizens to express their thanks. Legend also says a slave rode in the chariot with the general, purposely placed behind him, and continually whispered in the general's ear words that served to protect him from any delusions of grandeur that might arise as the people heralded his name in praise. Two words: *Memento mori* (pronounced *me-MEN-toh MOR-ee)*. Loosely translated this means, "Remember to die." Remember that you are a mortal seeking immortality: from dust you have come, and to dust you shall return. In Christian terminology, you exist to serve, not to be served.

Ironically, after the Eden transgression, servanthood is not how humans are programmed to behave. Instead, the moment we become aware of the possibility of death, we work diligently to survive. Life in general promotes selfishness: we began selfishly with a desire to be fed, to be cradled, and to be served. Such immature desires thrive in adolescence and remain into adulthood, with us trying desperately to avoid serving but eager to be served.

Early on, we live our lives as though we will live forever, and existence becomes a journey of acquiring more and more things, but somewhere along the way, hopefully, we realize that "more" turns out to never be "enough." Our desire for more is a stronger emotion than the satisfaction that comes with acquiring what it is we desire. We finish a meal and start planning the next. We no sooner return from vacation than we start dreaming of the next. We leave a party trying to figure out where to have our next. Solomon wrote about it: "Vanity of vanities, saith the Preacher, vanity of vanities; all is vanity" (Ecclesiastes 1:2). He repeats the phrase for emphasis of its significance.

We sometimes forget that, no matter what we have and who we are, we all will eventually die. And no matter how hard we try to live, we will die. But when we become a Christian, we realize there is a different approach to living. And we have multiple biblical examples that instruct us about life: how to live, but also, how to die.

Christ's teaching on this subject is our ultimate example:

> Then said Jesus unto his disciples, If any man will come after me, let him deny himself, and take up his cross, and follow me. For whosoever will save his life shall lose it: and whosoever will lose his life for

Memento Mori: Remember To Die

> my sake shall find it. For what is a man profited, if he shall gain the whole world, and lose his own soul? or what shall a man give in exchange for his soul?
>
> Matthew 16:24-26

Paul followed up with these words: "I am crucified with Christ: nevertheless I live; yet not I, but Christ liveth in me ... " (Galatians 2:20).

But these verses aren't speaking of literal death, they are speaking of a spiritual change and the lifestyle that follows: how we should live as Christians and how we are to serve Christ and our fellowman. Jesus said it succinctly: "But he that is greatest among you shall be your servant" (Matthew 23:11). We need this reminder hanging in a prominent place in our lives: Memento mori, remember to die.

We are oh so familiar with physical death, and we rightly abhor it, for it is the penalty of Adam's transgression passed down to all mortals. But this is not what Christ was referencing; instead, He spoke of a spiritual death. So, how do we die spiritually? We give up our right to live our lives as we choose, and we relinquish that choice to Christ: a total surrender of our will to the will of Jesus Christ. We become His servants, with no rights of our own; rather, we submit to Him as Lord and Master.

It is significant for Christians to understand the concept of servanthood. In Bible days, from which the idea of Christian service arrives, servants had no rights: a strange concept for many of us today. So, in a democratic, union-minded mentality, how do we develop a servant's heart? Like many Bible principles, we must first become aware, and sometimes we have to take baby steps in development. An excellent time and place to start begins at daybreak in the home. As soon as you awaken, remind yourself: "Memento mori ... remember to die to God's will today ... remember to serve." And practice it before you leave your room. Remind yourself you're a servant by making up your bed, instead of expecting a parent or a spouse to do this for you. Toss your pajamas in the clothes basket instead of on the floor. Wipe the water from off the sink counter after you wash your hands. And live all day accordingly: remembering that we are all dying men, and to die well in Christ is to have lived a servant's life. The list continues:

- When you're walking down the hallway at school or work and see a piece of paper on the floor: memento mori. Stoop, pick it up, and toss it in a garbage can.
- When you finish your lunch and notice litter on the lunch table: memento mori. Tidy-up the table.
- When someone treats you rudely by cutting line, instead of getting mad, remind yourself who you are and to Whom you belong: memento mori.
- When someone cuts you off on the freeway: memento mori.
- When you see a person needing assistance: memento mori.
- When God blesses you financially: memento mori.
- When volunteers are requested: memento mori.

Such action doesn't come naturally; contrariwise, the natural

Memento Mori: Remember To Die

tendency is resistance. Servanthood is a task we have to continually work at, for the human spirit, left unchecked, will default to its carnal nature: selfishness. Not my job description. I didn't hire in for that. My four and no more. And worse: me, myself, and I.

What situation are you going through right now? To facilitate a God-blessed outcome: memento mori. What unfairness are you enduring? To calm the anger that is boiling inside: memento mori. What friend has hurt you? To prevent bitterness that will eat away at your soul: memento mori. What task has God called you to fulfill, be it ever so humble? In order to please the Lord, we must operate with a servants heart: memento mori. Are you shutting people out, including God, as you try to find yourself? Some admonish, "You've got to think of you, what you want." How contrary to Scripture. Remember Christ's instruction: lose your life for His sake and you will find it. That's definitely a memento mori.

The city of Corinth, where Paul established a church, definitely lacked this quality of servanthood. In contrast, they were a prideful people. Three characteristics dominated the lives of these Greeks: intellectual arrogance, material affluence, and moral corruptness. Alexander and his army had conquered the known world, spreading Grecian influence everywhere their feet trod. And though Rome eventually prevailed over them, even as a conquered nation, the Grecian language still dominated, remaining the lingua franca, or the common language that bridged the countries of the Roman Empire. This cultural pride filtered into the church, prompting Paul to write a letter to them in which he rebuked them for their disunity and for their moral failures. Even though these were common, traditional traits, Paul reminded them, "What? know ye not that your body is the temple of the Holy Ghost which is in you, which ye have of God, and ye are not your own? For ye are bought with a price: therefore glorify God in your body, and in your spirit, which are God's" (1 Corinthians 6:19-20).

In times past the garment identified the servant. The Scripture admonishes the Christian in proper spiritual attire. "Likewise, ye younger, submit yourselves unto the elder. Yea, all of you be subject one to another, and be clothed with humility: for God resisteth the proud, and giveth grace to the humble" (1 Peter 5:5). When we wear the garment of humility, we live without undo expectations. God's gifts to us are more appreciated. We aren't offended so easily, for a servant has few expectations. Still, it is the pathway to elevation: "By humility and the fear of the Lord are riches, and honour, and life" (Proverbs 22:4).

At all times and in all circumstances, for us to live well is to have constant awareness of our position as a servant of Christ: memento mori. To be like Christ we must become servants. As a man, Christ abandoned His role of Deity and "... made himself of no reputation, and took upon him the form of a servant, and was made in the likeness of men" (Philippians 2:7). Service to Christ involves two areas. One, directly serving Him through worship, prayer, and deeds of service to His Kingdom. The second area is indirectly serving Christ by serving others. This parable of Christ says it well:

> Then shall the King say unto them on his right hand, Come, ye blessed of my Father, inherit the kingdom

Memento Mori: Remember To Die

prepared for you from the foundation of the world: For I was an hungred, and ye gave me meat: I was thirsty, and ye gave me drink: I was a stranger, and ye took me in: Naked, and ye clothed me: I was sick, and ye visited me: I was in prison, and ye came unto me. Then shall the righteous answer him, saying, Lord, when saw we thee an hungred, and fed thee? or thirsty, and gave thee drink? When saw we thee a stranger, and took thee in? or naked, and clothed thee? Or when saw we thee sick, or in prison, and came unto thee? And the King shall answer and say unto them, Verily I say unto you, Inasmuch as ye have done it unto one of the least of these my brethren, ye have done it unto me.

Matthew 25:34-40

And He who commanded us to serve will help us fulfill His will. Further, He will someday reward those who do so with this proclamation: "… Well done, thou good and faithful servant: thou hast been faithful over a few things, I will make thee ruler over many things: enter thou into the joy of thy lord" (Matthew 25:21).

No More Shame

Many Christians, though forgiven by the Lord, have never forgiven themselves. They live in shame over past mistakes, and they live under the condemnation of regrets. The problem? This sense of shame isolates them from the presence of God. They feel their worship to God is unacceptable, and they feel a sense of unworthiness to get involved in ministry. Their isolation reinforces their self-imposed guilt, and irony of ironies, they feel abandoned by the Lord: a self-inflicted punishment. It's a vicious cycle of guilt, repentance, shame, and back to guilt. This loop doesn't incorporate significant principles of Scripture such as: a clean slate; sins cast into the sea; no more condemnation. This progression of shame needs to be broken, and it can be broken. It's as simple as accepting the fact, since God has forgiven me, I should forgive myself.

Some shame is brought on by a chosen lifestyle, while some shame is brought on because of the acts of others. Consider some of those acts for which children had no choice regarding the matter but were left with an element of shame:
- A parent abandons a child to be raised by grandparents.
- A grieving child somehow feels responsible for the divorce of parents.
- A child is abused physically and verbally.

- A teenager is sexually assaulted by a family member.
- A child is raised in poverty and equates that poverty as a lack of self-worth.

And there is the endless list of foolish choices we make. But whether guilt from bad personal choices or as a result of others' misdeeds, the dynamics of guilt are similar. Yet either way, God cares, and He wants to forgive us and to rid us of our shame.

There is an Old Testament account of a beautiful young woman, Tamar, daughter of King David, who exemplifies self-imposed shame. She was violated by Amnon, her half-brother, even though she desperately pleaded with him to refrain from the heinous act of incest: "And I, whither shall I cause my shame to go?" (2 Samuel 13:13). She lived with negative questions dominating her future: How can I show my face in public? Did I do something that facilitated the attack? How can I rid myself of the shame? Such questions plagued her, though she was an unwilling participant in the crime. King David had sent Tamar to her brother's house to care for him, unaware Amnon had feigned sickness and plotted the rape. Though Tamar was innocent, the tragedy destroyed her future. Perhaps the way her culture viewed this event perpetuated her shame, but Jesus came out of that culture, and He viewed it differently. To a guilty woman He proclaimed: "Neither do I condemn thee ..." (John 8:11). Sadly, when similar scenarios happen today, too often the perpetrator feels no remorse, but the offended person bears shame in self-imposed guilt. Many—innocent and guilty—struggle with a negative past that holds them captive.

No More Shame

The New Birth experience is designed to change our image of our past. Paul wrote:

> Nor thieves, nor covetous, nor drunkards, nor revilers, nor extortioners, shall inherit the kingdom of God. And such were some of you: but ye are washed, but ye are sanctified, but ye are justified in the name of the Lord Jesus, and by the Spirit of our God.
>
> 1 Corinthians 6:10-11

However, this concept of forgiving self, referred to by Jesus as being born again, eludes many converts. Though the debt of sin is paid in full by Jesus Christ's death at Calvary, many live as if the blame and shame is forever. Someone defined the shame experienced by a Christian as being "a grudge you hold against yourself." Such self-imposed guilt steals the "joy of salvation" and often drives the individual deeper into shame, thus creating the possibility of multiple emotional issues.

When you, as a Christian, hold on to past failures (no matter how personally responsible you were for your failures), you are refusing to do for yourself what the Lord willingly has done for you: He has forgiven you. Yes, there are consequences for sin, but forgiveness cleans the slate as far as God is concerned regarding condemnation. His forgiveness is designed to remove the personally felt shame. Jesus explained this to the woman guilty of adultery when He expressed that He did not condemn her. Remember, He wrote in the sand; He did not chisel her sins in stone. He uses chalk on an erasable board, not a permanent marker. Further, forgiveness is essential for you to be whole in Christ and in the relationship Christ desires with you. It is the goal of the Lord for you to be an overcomer of sin, but it is also God's desire for you to forgive yourself for your failures and to let go of the shame.

If we do not practice forgiveness of personal failures, we may not practice forgiveness toward others: both are extremely important. Forgiveness of self is significant for one to react properly in dealing with others who have failed. Consider the parable of a servant whose debts were forgiven him by the king:

> Therefore is the kingdom of heaven likened unto a certain king, which would take account of his servants. And when he had begun to reckon, one was brought unto him, which owed him ten thousand talents. But forasmuch as he had not to pay, his lord commanded him to be sold, and his wife, and children, and all that he had, and payment to be made. The servant therefore fell down, and worshipped him, saying, Lord, have patience with me, and I will pay thee all. Then the lord of that servant was moved with compassion, and loosed him, and forgave him the debt. But the same servant went out, and found one of his fellowservants, which owed him an hundred pence: and he laid hands on him, and took him by the throat, saying, Pay me that thou owest. And his fellowservant fell down at his feet, and besought him, saying, Have patience with me, and I will pay thee all. And he would not: but went and cast him

No More Shame

into prison, till he should pay the debt. So when his fellowservants saw what was done, they were very sorry, and came and told unto their lord all that was done. Then his lord, after that he had called him, said unto him, O thou wicked servant, I forgave thee all that debt, because thou desiredst me: Shouldest not thou also have had compassion on thy fellowservant, even as I had pity on thee? And his lord was wroth, and delivered him to the tormentors, till he should pay all that was due unto him. So likewise shall my heavenly Father do also unto you, if ye from your hearts forgive not every one his brother their trespasses.

Matthew 18:23-35

Evidently, this servant did not understand how forgiveness was supposed to work. Though forgiven a large debt, found someone who owed him, but instead of passing on the act of forgiveness which he had received, he demanded full payment. When payment could not be made, he had the debtor cast into prison. The question I ask, "Did he forgive himself, or was he still reacting subconsciously as a man who owed a debt and unconsciously scrambled to pay such. The end result wasn't good. His master, upon hearing of this unkindness, changed his mind and demanded of him all that he previously owed: the debt which had been forgiven was brought back up. What a travesty! His shame resurfaces in full force.

Could it be that if we don't forgive ourselves, it is possible that multiple past failures will unconsciously reappear? Overwhelming guilt can drive one into the abyss of shame and regret, immobilizing the person from normal activities of life. Could failing to let go of guilt from past forgiven failures immobilize us spiritually?

So, what are we to do with our shame? Obviously, we are to let it go. But how? Recognize the full price paid at Calvary. Christ died to pay our debt of sin; He died in utter shame, unclothed and exposed in total indignity, to cloak our shamefulness of sin. Because of the shame He accepted, we have the right and responsibility to reject such in our lives. If we don't, our Lord suffered humiliation for us in vain. The Lord died to pay our debt of sin because He loved us, not because he pitied us. Because of His sacrificial death, our sins are forgiven. Likewise, because of the shame He endured, we do not have to live with shame. We can let it go! The debt is paid. Let our actions reflect our experience: Christ bore our shame so we do not have to do so.

The Apostle Paul (also called Saul, his Jewish name) wasn't your innocent altar boy. To the contrary, hardened by Pharisaical traditions, he became an avid persecutor of the first Christians, hunting down and arresting many, separating parents from children. The church historian, Luke, describes Paul's barbaric deeds: "As for Saul, he made havock of the church, entering into every house, and haling men and women committed them to prison" (Acts 8:3). To the surprise of all who knew him, by a miraculous conversion, Paul became a Christian. In his own words he describes his unworthiness: "For I am the least of the apostles, that am not meet to be called an apostle, because I persecuted the church of God" (1Corinthian 15:9). Yet he refused to allow shame to prevent him from taking the gospel

No More Shame

farther than any of the other Apostles. How did he overcome this obstacle of shame and become the most effective of the apostles? He gave his shame over to the shame bearer, the shame taker, the shame breaker. Instead of wearing the garment of shame, he clothed himself in the cloak of Christ's great love: "There is therefore now no condemnation to them which are in Christ Jesus, who walk not after the flesh, but after the Spirit" (Romans 8:1).

Too many Christians spend untold days wrestling with unearned guilt. All the while, Christ bore their shame with full intentions for Calvary to erase both sin and shame. To live in shame drains the life-giving joy of the redeemed. A Christian living in shame uses all their energy to just stay afloat, and they do so in a sea of condemnation.

A story in the Old Testament of another Saul offers further insight into this subject of letting go of shame. What started as a beautiful beginning for King Saul ended in total disaster. And it engulfed his family as well. Sadly, Saul's son, Jonathan, suffered the same tragedy as his father. Both died in the battle on Mount Gilboa. Upon hearing of the death of Saul and Jonathan, and fearing for the life of Jonathan's young son, Mephibosheth, one of the maids gathered the five-year-old child in her arms and fled. During this frantic dash to safety, she fell, accidentally crippling the child in both feet.

The child's name fit the description of what he became. Mephibosheth, ironically, means "from the mouth of shame." The child's name succinctly described his grandfather's failure. In exile, the servants of Jonathan raised the child in an isolated town called

Lo-debar, far from the reach of the new king, David. The name of this isolated town spoke of its insignificance: "no pasture," "no word," or "no communication." The lad was cut off from the crown and reduced to mere existence. He remained isolated, bearing the shame of a father and grandfather who died in defeat. The conquerors had displayed their mutilated corpses, shamefully hanging their headless bodies on the city wall.

The faithful maid raised Jonathan's son. Though taking care of his essential needs, she was unable to remove the inherited shame of his father, nor the shame of his crippled walk.

Years passed, and King David, in contemplation of his former friendship with Jonathan, inquired if anyone remained alive of his household. This question could have been interpreted incorrectly, thinking David wanted to kill any survivors of Saul's lineage, but David's motives were pure, and he discovered Mephibosheth, now a grown man, was still alive. He quickly commanded, " … fetch him … ." These words had been spoken before from the throne of Israel's king. Years prior, Saul had said this regarding David, as he searched far and wide to find him. "… for he shall surely die" (1 Samuel 20:31), Saul had commanded. But this time it was different: " … that I may shew the kindness of God unto him" (2 Samuel 9:3).

Mephibosheth came as was demanded of him, hobbling on his crippled feet. Upon entering the throne room, he fell at David's feet and pleaded, "What is thy servant, that thou shouldest look upon such a dead dog as I am?" (2 Samuel 9:8). He had lived with emotional and physical shame, assuming the shame of his father and

No More Shame

grandfather, and he expected to be treated according to this shame: "a dead dog." To his surprise, David explained, "I'm restoring to you your grandfather's land and servants, and you shall eat bread always at my table as one of my sons." No more shame!

Ironically, Saul of the New Testament was of the same tribe of Saul in the Old Testament: the tribe of Benjamin. Perhaps he was named after Israel's first King. The reign of Saul of the Old Testament began with great promise; it ended in utter shame. In contrast, the work of Saul of the New Testament began in shame as he persecuted Christians and approved of the stoning of Stephen; however, it ended in honor. The difference in the two? Their choices. Saul of old looked to a witch to ask the dead prophet Samuel to conjure him a future. Saul of the New Testament looked to Jesus to cloak his past with Calvary's sacrifice. And so, he was able to write: "... Whosoever believeth on him shall not be ashamed" (Romans 10:11). Calvary removes our shame. "Therefore if any man be in Christ, he is a new creature: old things are passed away; behold, all things are become new" (2 Corinthians 5:17).

Our Spiritual Defense System

> No weapon that is formed against thee shall prosper; and every tongue that shall rise against thee in judgment thou shalt condemn. This is the heritage of the servants of the Lord, and their righteousness is of me, saith the Lord.
>
> Isaiah 54:17

Israel, with assistance from the United States, developed what is commonly called an iron dome defense system that protects against the launching of enemy missiles into their country. An arrangement of highly sophisticated defensive batteries scattered throughout their nation is on alert. Each battery has three necessary components that operate in sequence. First, a radar detection unit picks up any missile launched toward their country. Second, a management center predicts where the rocket will land, and this center determines whether it should be intercepted or ignored. Finally, when needed, a launcher fires an interceptor missile at the incoming enemy projectile and destroys it in midair.

Likewise, God has given us, through His Word, a spiritual iron dome defense system. It is simple, yet most effective. Our weapon? Thanksgiving. The Scripture instructs us, "In every thing give thanks: for this is the will of God in Christ Jesus concerning you" (1 Thessalonians 5:18). Paul wrote these words to the church he had established in Thessalonica, a city of about two hundred thousand people, with a large Jewish community. During his second missionary journey, he spent three Sabbaths in the city, sharing the Gospel in the streets and the synagogue. The result was the conversion to Christianity of some Jews and many Gentiles, specifically, some chief women. Some Jewish individuals—non-believers regarding Christianity—stirred up the community against Paul and his fellow laborer, Silas. The persecution was so severe that the Thessalonian believers, fearing for Paul and Silas' safety, sent them away under the protection of the night.

Because Paul was forced to leave this young church so abruptly, he wrote them two letters to offer direction regarding their newfound faith. Included in the message are several instructions. The above-selected verse is one of those instructions. The directive, "in everything give thanks," is a difficult command to obey, for it goes against human nature, and thanksgiving sometimes takes much effort. However, this command to give thanks comes without qualification. We are to give thanks in every situation: the good and the bad.

Why should we give thanks for all things? Let's make sure we have read the Scripture correctly. The instruction was not to give thanks "for" all things; rather, we are to give thanks "in" all things, or we could say, "during all things."

Why give thanks during all things, including challenging

Our Spiritual Defense System

situations? This spiritual act of thanksgiving combines both faith and obedience in spite of the circumstances. Giving thanks acknowledges God's presence and proclaims His goodness even though you can't see, hear, or feel Him.

The giving of thanks is one of those spiritual principles of God which doesn't necessarily make sense to mankind. But God knows what works best, and so the Scripture proclaims: turn the other cheek; prefer your brother; the first shall be last and the last first; give liberally, and you can live better on what is left; we live because Christ died. Here's how the principle of thanksgiving works: we give thanks regardless of how we feel, and Christ gives us peace in spite of our circumstances.

A thankful heart becomes our spiritual iron dome defense system. It has three components:
- Thankfulness opens our hearts to God's presence. Surrounded by a hedge of God's protection, nothing can penetrate God's shield without His permission. Further, for every sacrifice we make, or for every burden we bear, there is a promise from Christ: "And every one that hath forsaken houses, or brethren, or sisters, or father, or mother, or wife, or children, or lands, for my name's sake, shall receive an hundredfold, and shall inherit everlasting life" (Matthew 19:29). We become the recipient of the gifts God desires and promises to give those who sacrifice for His cause.
- Thankfulness prevents fear that comes from the

adversary's accusations and opens our minds to God's thoughts. God thoughts are more significant than our problems, and when God thoughts consume us, there is little time left to worry. "For the which cause I also suffer these things: nevertheless I am not ashamed: for I know whom I have believed, and am persuaded that he is able to keep that which I have committed unto him against that day" (2 Timothy 1:12).

- Thankfulness opens our hearts to God's peace: "And the peace of God, which passeth all understanding, shall keep your hearts and minds through Christ Jesus" (Philippians 4:7). Thankfulness is a weapon to which Satan has no counteraction. When he sends his best shot, and you say, "Thanks, God," Satan doesn't know what else to send your way. Why waste ammunition on a target that won't surrender but considers to strike back with praise? Instead of crying "uncle," the Christian ushers in God's presence with "... the sacrifice of praise to God ..." (Hebrews 13:15). King David was a warrior; he knew about the guts and blood of hand-to-hand combat. But his strength was not found in physical ability; contrariwise, his being equipped for battle was a spiritual principle: "And now shall mine head be lifted up above mine enemies round about me: therefore will I offer in his tabernacle sacrifices of joy; I will sing, yea, I will sing praises unto the Lord" (Psalms 27:6).

Our Spiritual Defense System

As long as we protest, criticize, grumble, and whine, Satan knows where to direct his missiles of destruction. As long as we complain, Satan will keep lobbing rockets our way. When we start giving thanks, no other weapon is necessary for our defense, for "No weapon that is formed against thee shall prosper ..." (Isaiah 54:17). Satan doesn't know what to do against us when he unleashes a volley of firepower, but we, instead of kowtowing to his demands and accusations, stand to our feet and give God praise.

What attack are you experiencing right now? Give God thanks in spite of the circumstances. What bomb is the enemy hurling your way? Name it and give God thanks that He counts you worthy to endure. What bombardment has you hunkered down, afraid, or maybe ashamed to show your face? Crawl out of your bunker and shout your thanksgiving to the One Who sees, hears, and cares about your situation. Praise causes the enemy's tactics to backfire. And you'll begin to realize that the adversary hesitates in wasting ammo on a moving target: a target that won't stop praising God.

Renewing The Mind

British author Julian Barnes wrote: "You are what you have done; what you have done is in your memory; what you remember defines who you are ... ."[1] For too many, the past controls the present and dictates the future. Sadly, the memories of the past often predetermine the future.

It was his thirty-eight-year memory that held captive a disabled man at the pool of Bethesda (John 5:1-9). There were many diseased that day: "In these lay a great multitude of impotent folk, of blind, halt, withered, waiting for the moving of the water. For an angel went down at a certain season into the pool, and troubled the water: whosoever then first after the troubling of the water stepped in was made whole of whatsoever disease he had" (John 5:3-4). Jesus asked one of them, a lame man: "... Do you want to get well?" (John 5:6 NIV). It was a simple yes or no question regarding the moment, but the disabled man went into an essay regarding his past:
- I never have anyone to help me: blaming.
- As you can see, I am a cripple, and it always takes me too long to get to the pool when the angel stirs the water, so someone always gets there before me: self-pity.
- Last year it was a blind man—whose cousins helped him— who received a healing: complaining.

Over time, this man sank into the quagmire of a negative past, and his current condition justified his concession to the inevitable. Instead of miracles at the pool increasing his faith, they stole his hope for healing. He mulled over the disappointment that he wasn't the one who received a healing. Further, his particular disease dictated his inability to meet the requirements for healing: the one to step into the water first was healed. Consider how he may have interpreted the absurdity of Jesus' question: Since he couldn't walk, he wasn't a candidate for a miracle. No wonder the Apostle wrote: "And be not conformed to this world: but be ye transformed by the renewing of your mind, that ye may prove what is that good, and acceptable, and perfect, will of God" (Romans 12:2). God's will is not predicated upon who we are; rather, it is determined by Christ, Who is "... no respecter of persons" (Acts 10:34).

Herein lies the danger: we default to our old nature. The failures and fears and traumas of our past amplify the hopelessness of the present and prevent optimism for the future. In this stuck-state stage of mental despair, we focus on disappointments, broken trusts, abuses, a failed marriage, a business gone belly-up, an overbearing parent, an absent parent, addictions, and deep secrets of our soul. But the God of glory steps into our world and beckons us into His prepared future; instead of following Christ's purpose, we often cower in the corner of our past, failed experiences.

In a well-documented experiment, Steve Ramirez and Xu Liu, Doctorate students at MIT in Cambridge, have proven the power of memory—the past—to control our present. In an experiment, they implanted a lab mouse's memory within the brain of another

Renewing The Mind

lab mouse, and that memory controlled the present actions of the second mouse. In essence, the experimenters implanted memory cells of a bad experience by a mouse into a different mouse who did not have that experience. The details of their experiment were complex, but the outcome was rather simple: the traumatic memory cells of a mouse, injected into another mouse, literally controlled the immediate responses of the latter mouse, even though the memory cells were that of a completely different mouse.

In considering a spiritual analogy for this experiment, let's reflect upon how the Bible describes Satan: "… the accuser of our brethren…" (Revelation 12:10). The adversary of our soul exploits a memory that is contrary to our present status with Christ. That's how Satan works: always accusing, always bringing up the past. He plants negative seeds of thought regarding the past (whether true or false), reminding us of failures, sins, and misgivings. His goal is to keep us in a negative history, and if he can keep us in a negative past, our present will be miserable, and we will have no strength to progress toward the future. These continual antics of the adversary is a daily battle strategy of Satan. However, there is a way to override the past and live according to God's desired plan: a positive present and a promising future. God's word declares:

> For though we walk in the flesh, we do not war after the flesh: (For the weapons of our warfare are not carnal, but mighty through God to the pulling down of strong holds;) Casting down imaginations, and every high thing that exalteth itself against the knowledge of God, and bringing into captivity every

thought to the obedience of Christ.

2 Corinthians 10:3

Bringing into captivity our thoughts? That's what we need to work on: aligning our thoughts with the proclamation of Scripture. God's plan for our present life is not contingent on our past. We dare not dwell upon our history; instead, we should identify with the current strategy of God. How can we do this? Here are some directives:

- Acknowledge that God knows your every thought, and nothing hides from His omniscience, especially our sins. After you have confessed your sin, accept God's forgiveness and seek direction and strength to overcome the sin in the future.
- Parents, whether biological or spiritual mentors, should allow children to be honest with them and encourage them to be honest with God. Recognize that various temptations confront our youth every day, and a slew of emotions and hormones and biological changes—that they don't quite know how to explain—bombard them regularly. Get your head out of the sand and recognize that your children are not angels, but neither are they demons; instead, they are God's struggling creation. Your task? Communicate. Love them unconditionally but confront their immaturity and their sin. Do all you can to protect them from sensuality and the adversary of their soul by controlling what they watch, listen to, participate in, and the company they keep. The more junk you can prevent from getting into their lives, the less shame and negativism they will have to deal with in the

Renewing The Mind

future. Check their cell phones and iPads at random. As a parent, you have that God-given right and responsibility to offer guidelines in your home. You argue: "Such treatment may chase them away from God. Shouldn't I give them liberty to make such choices?" Rules and discipline should be administered with love, but consider that eighteen-year-old cadets are told when to go to bed, when to get up, how to make their beds, what to wear, etc. Still, they are expected to win wars. I think you get the picture.

- Recognize that the battlefield is the mind. Let your mantra become: I will not concede to the accusations of Satan. He is a liar, and he does not like me, nor is he looking out for my good; therefore, I will not cater to his accusations of my past. The only thing in the past that is significant for me is Calvary!

- Practice godly thoughts, heavenly thoughts, positive thoughts. One of the ways to do this is by quoting Scripture. What does the Bible say? "Thy word is a lamp unto my feet, and a light unto my path" (Psalms 119:105). Whether for the moment, or in the future, the Word of God illuminates our path. It doesn't matter what the past may have been, the Bible says I am forgiven. The Lord loves me. I am His child. "For ever, O Lord, thy word is settled in heaven" (Psalms 119:89). What does God's Word say about you? For you? To you? Quote these verses until your heart knows and believes them.

- Take charge of any negative thoughts that bring harm to your spiritual walk. This is done by replacing carnal thoughts with spiritual thoughts. Evidently, the church in Philippi was experiencing anxiety over some issue. In the closing lines of his letter to them, Paul admonished the church: "Be careful for nothing ..." (Philippians 4:6). Don't be anxious; instead, with a thankful heart take your concerns to the Lord in prayer. This brings peace to an anxious heart. "And the peace of God, which passeth all understanding, shall keep your hearts and minds through Christ Jesus" (Philippians 4: 7). This doesn't make sense to the carnal man, but it isn't designed to do such, it's God's plan for His own. But this peace can be interrupted by improper thoughts, so, Paul continued: "Finally, brethren, whatsoever things are true, whatsoever things are honest, whatsoever things are just, whatsoever things are pure, whatsoever things are lovely, whatsoever things are of good report; if there be any virtue, and if there be any praise, think on these things" (Philippians 4:8). By the way, do we know why the Philippians were so troubled? We do. Their beloved Paul was in prison. But from a prison cell, he offered these directions for a peaceful heart. And he reinforced the way to peace: "Those things, which ye have both learned, and received, and heard, and seen in me, do: and the God of peace shall be with you" (Philippians4: 9).

Jesus asked the disabled man, "Would you like to be healed?" The miracle worker stood before him, extending a hand for him to rise and walk, but the man's negative thought process almost cost him his miracle: blaming, self-pity, and complaining. What a tragedy that would have been!

Renewing The Mind

Why not stop making that same mistake today? Accept the final admonition of Paul: "But my God shall supply all your need according to his riches in glory by Christ Jesus" (Philippians 4:19). And answer in the affirmative Christ's question: "... Do you want to get well?" (John 5:6 NIV). Instead of excuse making, reflect the response of the two blind men who sought after Christ. No matter how difficult it was for them, they pressed through the crowd, ruffled feathers, tripped over cobblestones, and rounded corners following after the Lord until he entered a certain house. When Jesus questioned them, they responded affirmatively. "Believe ye that I am able to do this? ... Yea, Lord" (Matthew 9:28).

Two simple words made all the difference. "Yea, Lord." No excuses. No blaming. No complaining about their past. No self-pity. Just two words of faith that released the power of God into their lives. Yes, Lord. Much easier to say than a diatribe of excuses and complaints. And the rewards are awesome!

Endnote
1) Nothing to Be Frightened Of, Julian A. Barnes, Knopf, New York, 2008

Jesus The Giver: Satan The Taker

The vast majority of people, whether they acknowledge it or not, are servants to Satan. "Whoa!" you say. Now, I'm aware such a statement raises a lot of eye-brows and gets a lot of people worked into a frenzy. And some even dare use choice expletives to prove me wrong. And many who dare admit they are sinners and servants to Satan, fail to acknowledge that in the end, Satan cannot help them. And even if he could, he would not. Why? Two reasons: One, he hates God's creation with a passion, enough so that he delights in their eternal punishment. The second reason? He can't help anyone in the end, for this is his end: "And the devil that deceived them was cast into the lake of fire and brimstone, where the beast and the false prophet are, and shall be tormented day and night for ever and ever" (Revelation 20:10).

Yet no one has to serve Satan, for Christ made provision at Calvary to set all mankind free from Satan's dominion. But people still serve him: some because they enjoy sin, some out of deception, and some as if there is some advantage in doing so. They've experienced but part of a scriptural principle: "to enjoy the pleasures of sin" (Hebrews 11:25), but they aren't counting on the second part of that principle being enforced: "for a season." It's fun, but it's short lived, and then comes an eternity for which they haven't prepared. This causes me to consider how much Satan takes from mankind compared to how little he gives them in return for their service.

Consider this analogy of a bank statement I once received. In bold letters half-way down the page, the statement highlighted the word "Interest," and underneath the word it showed me how much I earned in interest for the previous month. I had made eight cents. Further, the statement shared how much it cost me to make those eight pennies: the service charge on my account for the month was eight dollars. You read the figures correctly! They charged me eight dollars to give me eight cents. That's a loss of one hundred times what I gained. Folks, any way you slice it, that's not a good deal. But that is the kind of deal Satan offers the masses. You give him your life, and he offers you a few moments of pleasure followed by eternal damnation: a bad deal.

Christ's temptation by Satan is a prime example of the deals Satan promotes. To get a better idea of what took place, we need to establish the full picture of the Bible account. Consider these Scriptures as a setting: "In the beginning was the Word, and the Word was with God, and the Word was God. The same was in the beginning with God. All things were made by him; and without him was not any thing made that was made ... and the Word was made flesh" (John 1:1-3,14). The Scripture establishes that the Word, which was God, became a man in Christ Jesus. Therefore, Jesus was more than a man: He was also God. Consider further what the Scripture says about Christ as Creator: "For by him were all things created, that are in heaven, and that are in earth, visible and

Jesus The Giver: Satan The Taker

invisible, whether they be thrones, or dominions, or principalities, or powers: all things were created by him, and for him" (Colossians 1:16). From this Scripture we establish that Jesus—as God—created the world. So, we can deduce from Scripture that the world, at the time of Christ's temptation, already belonged to Him.

Now, take a look at Satan's offer:

> And the devil, taking him up into an high mountain, shewed unto him all the kingdoms of the world in a moment of time. And the devil said unto him, All this power will I give thee, and the glory of them: for that is delivered unto me; and to whomsoever I will I give it. If thou therefore wilt worship me, all shall be thine.
>
> Luke 4:5-7

Satan offered Jesus something he couldn't give Him: the world. Further, he offered Christ the world without the cross: without suffering. But though he offered Christ something he could not deliver, he demanded the ultimate price from Christ: worship. Even though the world is not Satan's to give away, he still offers the same to us today: the world at our feet. I'm not sure what Satan is offering you in the world, but I know what it will cost you! It will cost you far more than you will receive. It will cost you your best and most cherished possessions. How do I know this? It's his nature: Satan is not a giver; he is always a taker.

A cute folktale says it well:

Said the scorpion to the turtle, "Hey, friend, how about a lift across the river?" Whereupon the turtle responded, "Surely not, old fellow, for I fear you'd sting me along the way, and I'd drown." To which the scorpion argued, "Now that wouldn't make any sense at all, for if I stung you, and you drowned, I'd drown, too." And since the scorpion's logic made sense, the turtle agreed to give him a lift. But sure enough, about half-way across the river, the scorpion lifted his tail and jabbed his stinger into the turtle's head. As the turtle plunged to the bottom of the river, never to rise again, he craned his neck to see the scorpion frantically clinging to his back, whereupon he shouted to the scorpion, "Now that wasn't logical. You've killed us both." But the scorpion responded with a frown, "It has nothing to do with logic, it's just my stinking nature."[1]

And so it is with Satan: his is a nature to always take. Consider these Bible examples of Satan's bad deals offered to others:
- Adam and Eve: What did he give? One bite of fruit from the forbidden tree. What did he take? Their innocence, their relationship with God, their home, their future, their firstborn son's fellowship, their second born son's life, and eventually theirs.
- Job: What did Satan give? Sores, insomnia, pain, and sorrow. What did he take? Everything but Job's life and the life of his depressed wife. Some have even suggested Satan left her alive knowing her grieving

Jesus The Giver: Satan The Taker

    would complicate Job's pain.
- Prodigal son: What did he take? He took his entire inheritance. What did he give? He gave him a job slopping the hogs.

Satan is a taker, but God is a giver! "The thief (Satan) cometh not, but for to steal, and to kill, and to destroy: I am come that they might have life, and that they might have it more abundantly" (John 10.10).

In stark contrast, Jesus is a giver. Consider these Bible examples of His blessings:
- To a young woman taken in adultery, the world had said, "Sin is fun." But in the end, what did it give her? Threats from men with rocks drawn to hurl at her. And they would have taken her life, but Jesus had a plan called grace. He extended mercy. "Neither do I condemn thee: go, and sin no more" (John 8.11), Jesus said to her after He had sent her accusers scrambling for anonymity.
- To an elderly woman taken over by a spirit of infirmity, Jesus challenged her invisible attacker. She was bent at the waist by a spirit of infirmity (an evil spirit using a physical condition as a means of torture). The enemy had literally attacked her body. We are not sure how or when, or if she had given in to this evil spirit, but Jesus doesn't cast you aside even if you have given yourself over to a sin and Satan. He seeks to set you free. He said, "Thou art loosed" (Luke 13.12), and she stood straight as smoothly as the words flowed from His lips.

How can we ward off the evil offerings of Satan and receive the blessings of God? We have to learn to say no to Satan and yes to Jesus. Here's a simple example:

- Satan says, "You shouldn't go to church because you need your rest so you can work and make money." So, you skip church and go to work the next day. You are all rested and ready to work when the boss says, "The electricity is shut off, so, we can't work this shift. Go home and rest. Maybe we'll work tomorrow." The enemy stole your worship, and circumstances took your work.
- Of this same scenario, Jesus says, "Go to church and I will supply you with enough energy to work." So, you go to church. The next day you are tired, but you go to work anyway. The boss says, "I like your work ethic. You're always here and always on time. I'm going to give you a raise to reward your benefit to the company." You gave your time to Christ, and He nudged your boss to give you a raise.

Satan is a taker: Jesus is a giver.

- Satan says, "Withhold your tithe or you won't have enough money to buy gasoline for the car, and you won't be able to get to work, and if you don't work you won't have any money to give to the church." So, you give only a part of the tithe. The next day, you go to your car to drive to work, but your car won't start. It takes your gasoline money to fix it. You don't make it to work on Monday. The church

Jesus The Giver: Satan The Taker

lost your tithe, you lost your gasoline money, and the adversary won again.
- Of this same scenario, Jesus says, "Honor me with your tithe on Sunday, and I will make a way for you where there seems to be no way." So, in spite of your limited finances, you give your tithe anyway. The next day, you go to your car to drive to work and your car won't start. "Jesus," you ask, "where are you?" He may seem silent, but just then a friend comes by and says, "What's wrong?" You say, "My car won't start." He says, "I can fix it." You ask, "How much money?" He says, "I'll do it for free, because I'm your friend."

Satan is a taker, but Jesus is a giver.

Many times we don't necessarily realize His gifts, but we facilitate His benefits by exemplifying trust in His character and faithfulness to His Word. We dare not allow the devil to deceive us into thinking God doesn't care about us as individuals. Jesus cares very much about what we are going through right now. He wants to help us through our personal problems, our children's problems, our work problems, our financial problems, our health problems, and our emotional problems. However, it is important that we incorporate trust in our approach to God. Such trust helps us become faithful to however His Word instructs us to live. But how do we trust God? By our attitude, our actions, and our verbalizations.
- We worship Him when we don't know how we are going to make it.

- We remain faithful when things are not going well.
- We take time to pray and read our Bible every day, even though we feel we are too busy to do so.
- We come to church when we are sad, when we are discouraged, and even when it may seem we have more important things to do.
- We move beyond being a spectator, and we become a participator in worship.

Jesus is a giver. Consider the gifts Christ offers us:
- Forgiveness: He takes away our sins at baptism. Through baptism we identify with His death on the cross. When we sin after baptism, He takes away our sins when we sincerely repent.
- The Holy Spirit baptism: This gift is joy indescribable, and the experience is higher than any high imaginable. It has no negative side effects but is full of lasting benefits: strength to overcome; wisdom beyond years; passion to help others; courage to share the gospel; resurrection power to take us to heaven.
- A clear conscience: He gives calm regarding our past as if it never happened, and He gives understanding so we do not repeat our mistakes.
- Hope: Christ offers expectations for tomorrow when all looks hopeless.
- Peace: He takes away our fears and replaces them with comfort and direction.

What should we do to receive such gifts that Christ desires

Jesus The Giver: Satan The Taker

to give unto us? Some say, "Just have faith and it will eventually happen." But this is but partial truth: faith needs to be defined. From a biblical perspective, unless God demands of us to "do nothing" to show our faith, faith tends to involve participation by the believer. "Ask, seek and knock," Jesus explained (Matthew 7:7-9). These are all action words. We dare not sit around wistfully hoping—and ultimately complaining—when nothing good happens.

Faith says we should claim the promises with spiritual awareness and with specific actions. By faith Noah "... prepared an ark ...." (Hebrews 11:7). By faith Abraham "... obeyed; and he went out, not knowing whither he went" (Hebrews 11:8). Faith is "... works in action," James explained (James 2:18), not sitting around thumb twiddling. Receiving the promises of Christ is not for the inactive. The lame man at the Pool of Bethesda almost missed his miracle because of his passivity (John 5). Circumstances had taken away his quality of life; the thief had left him an invalid for thirty-eight years, but Jesus had a gift for him that day. Jesus proclaimed, " ... Rise, take up thy bed, and walk" (John 5:8). Thankfully, after an obvious excuse, he did.

Do you desire the gifts Christ offers? Then it's time to stand for God, stand against the enemy, and demand the adversary leave— through the authority in Jesus' name. It's time to triumphantly proclaim victory through the promises of Scripture. It's time to worship as if the gift has already been given. In the process, you will be the recipient of the gifts that Jesus wants to give. This is His promise: "If ye then, being evil, know how to give good gifts unto your children, how much more shall your Father which is in heaven give good things to them that ask him" (Matthew 7:11).

Satan is a taker (that's his stinking nature); conversely, Jesus is a giver. And that is His loving nature.

Endnote
1) This story has multiple sources, so the author is uncertain of its origin

Suffering With Purpose

For unto you it is given in the behalf of Christ, not only to believe on him, but also to suffer for his sake.
Philippians 1:29

When Jesus came into the coasts of Caesarea Philippi, he asked his disciples, saying, Whom do men say that I the Son of man am? And they said, Some say that thou art John the Baptist: some, Elias; and others, Jeremias, or one of the prophets. He saith unto them, But whom say ye that I am? And Simon Peter answered and said, Thou art the Christ, the Son of the living God. And Jesus answered and said unto him, Blessed art thou, Simon Barjona: for flesh and blood hath not revealed it unto thee, but my Father which is in heaven. And I say also unto thee, That thou art Peter, and upon this rock I will build my church; and the gates of hell shall not prevail against it. And I will give unto thee the keys of the kingdom of heaven: and whatsoever thou shalt bind on earth shall be bound in heaven: and whatsoever thou shalt loose on earth shall be loosed in heaven. Then charged he his disciples that they should tell no man that he was Jesus the Christ. From that time forth began Jesus to shew unto his disciples, how that he must go unto Jerusalem, and suffer many things of the elders and chief priests and scribes, and be killed, and be raised again the third day. Then Peter took him, and began to rebuke him, saying, Be it far from thee, Lord: this shall not be unto thee. But he turned, and said unto Peter, Get thee behind me, Satan: thou art an offence unto me: for thou savourest not the things that be of God, but those that be of men. Then said Jesus unto his disciples, If any man will come after me, let him deny himself, and take up his cross, and follow me. For whosoever will save his life shall lose it: and whosoever will lose his life for my sake shall find it.

Matthew 16:13-25

The Lord complimented the Apostle Peter for recognizing His deity; conversely, Christ called him Satan for failing to realize the humanity of Christ demanded that He experience suffering. Still, we can sympathize with Peter, for the message of suffering brings more questions than answers:

- Is suffering an indication I'm out of God's will?
- I hear testimonies of the victories of others, but why has God not healed me?
- Is my suffering of my own doing?
- Is it punishment for some secret sin?
- Why hasn't my deliverance come?
- Am I insignificant in God's sight?

Suffering With Purpose

Mark Batterson, in his inspirational book, *The Circle Maker*, offers keen insight into this emotional battle.

> "Sometimes when you hear answers to prayer that others have experienced, it can be discouraging instead of encouraging because you wonder why God has answered their prayers but not yours. But let me remind you that these answers have rarely happened as quickly or easily as they sound. There is usually a backstory. So, we are quick to celebrate the answer to prayer, but the answer probably didn't come quickly. I've never met a person who didn't experience some big disappointments on the way to his or her big dream."[1]

Why suffering? The question is asked often and the answers can be quite perplexing. But for the Christian seeking a solution from Scripture, the answer can be simplified: it is the consequence of living in a fallen world. "These things I have spoken unto you, that in me ye might have peace. In the world ye shall have tribulation: but be of good cheer; I have overcome the world" (John 16.33).

As a rule of thumb, God doesn't cause our suffering. There are a few exceptions, but our loving Lord cares about our suffering. God allowed Job's suffering for some reason, reasoning which He withheld, even from Job, but all along, God cared about Job. God may not send problems to us, but when we suffer, He brings purpose to our pain. We may never realize the specifics, but God has a unique way of allowing suffering to serve a meaningful purpose in His

Kingdom and our personal lives.

It is no coincidence that Paul wrote to the church at Philippi regarding suffering. Upon receiving a vision from the Lord, Paul redirected his missionary journey from Asia into the region of Macedonia (northern Greece). Paul and Silas took the first available ship and sailed on the winds of confidence. "And after he had seen the vision, immediately we endeavoured to go into Macedonia, assuredly gathering that the Lord had called us for to preach the gospel unto them" (Acts 16:10). Surely, only victories awaited. Not so.

At Philippi, their ministry began with great promise. The conversion of the household of Lydia brought much joy. Shortly after this victory, Paul commanded an evil spirit to depart from a young woman. Revival had undoubtedly come to town, but in a matter of hours, this red-hot revival came to a screeching halt. Evil men—who used the young woman's fortune-telling abilities for personal gain—became extremely angry at Paul. Since she could no longer divine fortunes through an evil spirit, overnight these men lost their lucrative source of income. These spiritual pimps stirred up their Gentile customers against these meddling Christians and had Paul and Silas arrested and thrown in jail. In a short time frame we see the miraculous manifestation of God's power to deliver reversed by evil injustice, and the outcome includes a vicious beating and incarceration for Paul and Silas.

It was not a casual flogging. The Bible expresses they "laid many stripes upon them" (Acts 16:23). A whipping by Gentile

Suffering With Purpose

authorities could be cruel. In contrast, Jewish law regarding beatings as punishment forbid more than thirty-nine lashes. This was not so in Roman law; it depended upon the judge—or the mood of the one carrying out the sentence. From recorded Scripture, there was a lot of emotion involved in this particular judgment of Paul and Silas, and we can assume the beating was quite inhumane. Interestingly, Paul did not at this time inform them of his Roman citizenship and his legal rights for a fair trial, though he did during a later altercation (Acts 16:37).

Why didn't God intervene on behalf of Paul and Silas to prevent the arrest. Or prevent the beating? And imprisonment? We can only speculate. I don't think God necessarily wanted them to be beaten and cast into prison, but once the events transpired, God refused to allow such suffering to be wasted. He quickly assembled a plan.

But God needs us to cooperate when He creates a game plan. Paul and Silas could have been angry and blamed God for allowing such mistreatment. Instead, they joined with God to let their pain have meaning. At midnight, with beaten and bleeding backs and pain-racked bodies, they sang praises unto God. Suddenly, the miraculous happened: an earthquake shook the prison, and the doors burst open. Part one!

The jailer, thinking the prisoners had escaped and thus he would be executed for dereliction of duty, drew his sword to commit suicide, but Paul intervened. Part two!

Instead of the jailer taking his own life, he and his entire family accepted baptism into Christ. Part three! And what a miracle! Ironically, Paul and Silas didn't receive healing for their wounds; instead, the jailer tended to them by washing their open stripes.

Later on, the Philippian church was distressed when they heard Paul was again incarcerated. Perhaps some had forgotten the backstory, so in a letter to them, Paul reminded the believers how their church was founded: through suffering—his suffering. This was the background story. He encouraged them that some good would come from his prison captivity.

> But I would ye should understand, brethren, that the things which happened unto me have fallen out rather unto the furtherance of the gospel; So that my bonds in Christ are manifest in all the palace, and in all other places; And many of the brethren in the Lord, waxing confident by my bonds, are much more bold to speak the word without fear.
>
> Philippians 1:12-14

God doesn't allow pain to happen without giving it purpose. A host of Bible characters suffered much, but through their suffering, they advanced God's Kingdom. God didn't approve of what Joseph's brothers did to him. And Joseph's heart broke at the hardness of the hearts of his brothers toward him. One of the saddest Scriptures in the Bible is the description of Joseph as a servant: "... Joseph, who was sold for a servant: Whose feet they hurt with fetters: he was laid in iron" (Psalms 105:17-18). But God didn't waste such suffering. In fact, in His omniscience, God saw the tragedy before it

Suffering With Purpose

happened. "Moreover he called for a famine upon the land: he brake the whole staff of bread. He sent a man before them, even Joseph ..." (Psalms 105:16-17). And before God was finished, Joseph became second in power to the Pharaoh and ultimately saved his people from starvation.

The invading Babylonians hauled Daniel off into captivity at a young age. Separated from family and homeland the rest of his life, he survived captivity to serve under three kings, being a critical factor in Judah's survival as a people in exile. And he was one of the few prophets who saw the distant future, even the end of the ages.

Young David ran for his life from the wrath of jealous King Saul. The Judean wilderness could have drained his soul of spirit, but under the inspiration of the Holy Spirit he blesses us even today as we read from the Psalms which he wrote, sometimes while in utter despair.

We are well aware of what suffering does "to" us, but we sometimes overlook what personal suffering does "for" us.
- It drives us to our knees, which carries us into the presence of our Lord.
- It toughens us for future battles that could otherwise destroy us.
- It strengthens our resolve to trust God's Word.
- It teaches us patience: a very important virtue.
- It becomes rungs on the spiritual ladder to heights God desires to take us.
- It empties us of pride: one of the sins God hates.

- It affirms God's Word to us.
- It makes us passionate toward others who suffer.
- It removes us from the throne of self-sufficiency and ushers us into the throne-room of God.
- It often gives us a wonderful testimony of God's love and grace.

Consider what I call pre-suffering by studying the life of Joseph in the Old Testament. I tend to see an element of immaturity or silly pride in his life—his life before his suffering. Dressed in his snuggly coat-of-many-colors, he seemed proud to share with his brothers a dream of them bowing before him. One can never reach God's potential for them without some element of suffering. Post-suffering is different. When Joseph finally identified himself to his brothers in Egypt, it was because he desired reunion with them. It had nothing to do with reigning over them. He was stripped of any pride he may previously have had; he was overwhelmed with joy of being reunited with family.

There is a before and after state of suffering: "But the God of all grace, who hath called us unto his eternal glory by Christ Jesus, after that ye have suffered a while, make you perfect, stablish, strengthen, settle you" (I Peter 5:10). These positive qualities are the result of suffering, not succeeding.

I see the "before" and "after" suffering in one of the Psalms: "If it had not been the LORD who was on our side, now may Israel say; If it had not been the LORD who was on our side, when men rose up against us" (Psalms 124:1-2). Note the part, "now may Israel say."

Suffering With Purpose

Is that a hint that they recognized the Lord's hand more significantly after they had gone through some trials and tribulations of suffering?

Suffering is inevitable for anyone in this world. So, since we must suffer, we dare not waste our purpose by fighting against the pain, loss, and disappointment. We dare not fight against God's fire; conversely, we should let it consume the dross and make us better. We need to live with expectancy that God will bring some good out of our suffering.

- We can "curse the darkness or light a candle,"[2] as they say, and enjoy a good book while we wait.
- We can hunker down and endure the freezing winter or we can bundle up, put on ice skates, and dance across the frozen pond.
- We can loathe the pain or we can look for the forming pearl.
- We can allow suffering to get us down or we can let God bring down heavenly purpose and thus give the suffering some positive meaning.

Andrew and Bethany, a young couple in our church, have seen an unusual amount of suffering. They lost their first child shortly after birth to complications caused by human error. Their second child, Landon, has spinal muscular atrophy. The past twelve years have been full of trips to, and extended stays at, a hospital ninety miles away. In what could have destroyed their faith in God, they not only bore their burden gracefully, they allowed purpose to accompany the suffering. Instead of complaining about the long drive to the hospital, they thanked God that a hospital so close specialized in the disease their son has. They have become foster parents to other children in need. Their life and attitude have inspired many. Landon, lying on his back in his wheelchair, is positively touching more lives than we realize. God did not bring about his condition, but God is not wasting it without giving it meaning. Just this week, I sat across the desk from a banker who reminded me that God doesn't waste suffering. I had no idea she knew my association with Andrew and Bethany, so it surprised me when she said, "You have some of the sweetest people who attend your church. I met the young couple who has the boy in a wheelchair. That child is so inspiring!"

God hasn't wasted Landon's suffering—nor Andrew and Bethany's suffering. Nor is He wasting yours. Remember the opening Scripture? "For unto you it is given in the behalf of Christ, not only to believe on him, but also to suffer for his sake" (Philippians 1:29). Paul wrote these from a prison cell in Rome. While he awaited trial, Paul reminded the Philippian church that by design, the Gospel includes suffering, but suffering is not without purpose. God does not waste suffering.

Endnotes
1) Mark Batterson, The Circle Maker, Zondervan, Grand Rapids, MI, 2011, 78-79
2) William L. Watkinson, A sermon titled The Invincible Strategy, 1907

That All May Know

... that all the earth may know that there is a God in Israel.

I Samuel 17:46

Whether one recognizes it or not, no matter who we are or where we are from, there is a connection in all of our lives. We all are connected to each other via God, our Creator. We all come from a single ancestry: made by God, in the image of God (Genesis 1:27). However, we have not all acknowledged nor submitted to God. Thus, we do not necessarily acknowledge our connection with God or one another; therefore, we are divided by race, ethnicity, and language. God has done and is doing His part to fix this problem. Faith is our connection to God, and it is ultimately our connection to one another.

Faith is given to each of us in some measure, else we would have no connection to God. Many act upon this measure of faith, and the exercise of faith strengthens faith. We can allow the measure of faith God gives us to remain dormant. We can even discard faith altogether by rejecting God and the Bible. This was the case with many in the Old Testament era. Mankind severed his relationship with God to the point that he absolutely did not believe in God. "Because that, when they knew God, they glorified him not as God, neither were thankful; but became vain in their imaginations, and their foolish heart was darkened … . And even as they did not like to retain God in their knowledge, God gave them over to a reprobate mind, to do those things which are not convenient" (Romans 1:21,28). In contrast, we have Bible characters who grew their faith. How? We activate faith by acknowledging God's existence. We cultivate faith by seeking after God through prayer, studying the Bible, spending time alone in His presence, and participating in multiple moral activities.

God has a purpose in all of our lives: He has a plan for each of us to live for Him. The psalmist said it well: "I was cast upon thee from the womb: thou art my God from my mother's belly" (Psalms 22:10). Between God's plan for our lives and our realizing that plan, lots of things happen. Circumstances can take us away from God. At times we may walk in rebellion. We fail to believe God has called us, but God's call is like a bloodhound in chase: He is relentless. Though we have distanced ourselves, God has not distanced Himself. We can run from God like Jonah did, but we can't hide from Him, for He sees us in our hiding places just like He saw Jonah in the belly of the fish.

There is a pattern throughout Scripture of how relationships with God and man should work. God calls, we respond in a positive way, God responds to us. Consider these examples:
- The Flood: God called Noah, and he responded by spending a year building a boat that saved him and his family while the world perished. (Genesis 6-8)
- The Exodus: God called Moses, he delivered God's

That All May Know

message to Pharaoh. The Israelites responded by participating in the first Passover, exiting Egypt, and journeying toward the promised land. (Exodus 3-12)

- The Battle of Jericho: The Israelites had to shut their mouths, march around the walls daily for six days and seven times on the seventh day. They then shouted with a voice of triumph. God caused the walls of the city to fall down, and Israel prevailed in battle. (Joshua 6)
- The woman with an incurable disease: She pressed through the crowd and touched the hem of Christ's garment. Jesus noticed, and her act of faith in Him made her well. (Mark 5, Luke 8)
- The healing of the blind man: Jesus could have simply spoken healing, and it would have happened. Instead, he made mud cakes and put the mud on the man's eyes, then directed him to go to the Pool of Siloam and wash the mud from his eyes. He did. Only then did God heal him. (John 9)

Let's give further consideration to this last example. In between this blind man receiving directions from Christ to wash in the pool of Siloam and his actual washing, a lot of things could have happened. There were obvious roadblocks, stumbling stones, obstacles, and possibly detours. Consider all the things this man had to endure to receive the promise:

- The cobblestone terrain: It was rough maneuvering for a blind man (the crowded streets of Jerusalem could have easily gotten him off course).

- Jeers from the crowd: What might some have said to him along the way? "Is that mud in your eyes?" "Hey, Bro, is your mascara running?" "Nice shades."
- Surroundings: What about the dogs nipping at his heels and thieves trying to steal his few coins?
- Emotions: What mixed voices spoke into his head?

Still, he went, he washed, and he came back seeing! Obedient faith.

The dynamics of this story are the same in our lives. Between us and God are the obstacles of life. God calls us, and from that moment to where He desires to take us, there are lots of things that stand in our way. Situations happen that become a hindrance to us giving our hearts to God. Even when we make a start for God, some issues in life may actually get worse. We see this in the account of God appearing to Moses in a burning bush (Exodus 3). God called to him from the bush. Once Moses acknowledged, God told him to go back to Egypt and demand that Pharaoh release the Hebrews. But then God admonished him: Pharaoh will not let them go. The enemy always pushes back, even though God is leading the charge. Things got worse in Egypt before they got better. But God made a promise contingent upon Moses obeying: "... ye shall spoil the Egyptians" (Exodus 3:22). Victories are seldom problem free.

After Calvary, God calls all mankind to His side: "Now is the judgment of this world: now shall the prince of this world be cast out. And I, if I be lifted up from the earth, will draw all men unto me. This he said, signifying what death he should die" (John 12: 31-33).

That All May Know

While some haven't begun the designated journey, others haven't yet made it to the pool of promise. Some have been sidetracked by the roadblocks of difficulties. Some are interested but haven't experienced water baptism nor Holy Spirit baptism: the essentials of the New Birth experience to usher us into Christ's Kingdom, as explained by Christ to Nicodemus (John 3).

Like the blind man, some can't see their way through their problems: a disappointing job situation, a failing marriage, a sinful habit. But remember, God is not the one that is blind. He sees the way clearly. He is leading you to the pool of promise. Let go of your fear and take hold of His hand—obedient trust.

Some men have the idea that being a Christian takes away from their manliness; suggesting Christianity is for wimps. Or it's a crutch for the emotionally weak, so says the intellectual elite. These concepts are the farthest thing from the truth. One only has to consider Scripture to recognize that the men who lived for God and were written about in Scripture were anything but wimps and weaklings. They were:

- Courageous: This doesn't mean you're without fear; rather, you act in spite of your fear. Gideon, in spite of his misgivings, defeated a massive army with only three hundred men (Judges 6), simply because he obeyed God.
- Hard workers: Nehemiah directed the rebuilding of the wall around Jerusalem in fifty-two days (Nehemiah 6:15). That took a lot of push.
- Industrious: King Hezekiah orchestrated the building

of a huge, curving tunnel through stone to control the water supply inside the walls of Jerusalem. Two teams started at opposite ends and met in the middle, creating a continual slope to carry the water for a distance of five hundred eighty-three yards.
- Adventurous: Moses led some three million slaves through a wilderness for forty years.
- Skilled: Noah was a man who evidently excelled in math and carpentry.
- Resourceful: Abraham was a successful businessman although uprooted from familiar surroundings and a foreigner in a strange land.
- Influential: Job was the most influential and wealthiest man in the land.

Many were unlikely candidates to fulfill God's plan, yet they obeyed God in spite of their circumstances, and God used them for His purpose. David was an unlikely person to challenge Goliath. He was a song writer, harpist, sheep herder, and just a youth; yet we see him running onto the battlefield to face the warrior giant, his weapon a sling and five stones. Just a fairy tale, some say, it could not have literally happened. Their only arguments being their disbelief in Scripture. They don't believe the story, so it couldn't be true. But the book they are arguing against has survived the ages, and as time passes, more and more of its questionable contents are proven by archaeology to be true. Case in point: Some argued David was a fictitious character because of the lack of archaeological evidence. More recently, archaeologists uncovered a stone with David's name inscribed upon it. Yes, there was a King David.

That All May Know

Why would David go up against a seasoned warrior with a slingshot? Some things don't always make sense to the normal manner of thinking. Let me try and put this into perspective.

A few days ago, I overheard a conversation of a lady mailing a package via the US Postal Service. I wasn't sure who it was being mailed to, but I knew what it was that was being mailed: it was a box of Cheez-Its. It was not just a box that had contained Cheez-Its at some point in time; it was an unopened box of Cheez-Its to which she had attached a mailing label. The cost to mail the box was over six dollars. Teasingly, the mail clerk told her if she opened the box and ate a couple ounces of the Cheez-Its, it would be a lot cheaper to mail the box. We got a chuckle, but undeterred, the lady paid the full amount. Why would she mail a box of Cheez-Its? Couldn't the person receiving the package go to a store and purchase them cheaper? Was it an inside joke? What was the "why" behind this what? There was a reason, a connection I did not find out, but I can assume it was something tied to the heart or emotion or experience in life of the sender and the receiver. It was an action that made sense to that lady, and it probably made sense to the receiver; however, it made no sense to the clerk or those around her.

Why did young David do what one of the seasoned warriors of Israel should have done? David wasn't a warrior; rather, he was a lad, a harpist, and a sheep herder. It didn't make sense for him to march out onto the battlefield. And no one asked him to do so. No one commissioned him to go up against a giant. What prompted him? Why did he even think of doing such an unheard of act?

David's actions were deeper than impressing his brothers or trying to curry favor with King Saul. The situation was too serious for a show-off. For some, including his brothers, David's actions were as perplexing as the actions of the lady mailing a box of Cheez-Its, but they were clear to him. It seemed absurd to some that a shepherd boy challenge a seasoned bully and the very idea of such angered Goliath. But Goliath found out too late that he highly underestimated the lad's motives. David knew exactly why he accepted Goliaths challenge, and his actions had clarity of purpose. His reasoning? Simple. "...that all the earth may know that there is a God in Israel" (1 Samuel 17:46). Note, not a God in heaven but a God in Israel. That's personal!

Strangely, three thousand years later, like King Saul and his army, we're still hanging out on the battlefield of uncertainty. And mankind needs to know that God still reigns from on high and is concerned about what happens low—in our lives. Ironically, in dealing with our world, the God of the universe generally works through mere mortals: a youth with a sling; a lad with a small lunch-basket; a young servant girl in heathen captivity. Yes, you and me. If we fail, how will the world know?

Without being pretentious, when we engage with others—at work, at play, at home, at school, at a restaurant—let's seek to reflect our God in heaven. What is our box of Cheez-Its that is making others curious? A smile? A "Thank you" or "You can go ahead of me" comments? Simple things make all the difference. Are we practicing godly characteristics that leave the crowd wondering about us—in a positive way—to the point that they might just blurt

That All May Know

it out: "Who are you? What is it about you that makes me want to be around you?" We can.

Let our presence in the workplace or the store where we shop or any room we enter, cause a breath of hope to others? How did the prophet put it? In the middle of a thought, seemingly unrelated to the subject, he exclaimed: "... O Immanuel" (Isaiah 8:8): meaning, God with us! No matter the circumstances, God is present with us. Not only is God in heaven, He is with us! And when we are among family, friends, or even a stranger, we bring God to them. And when we depart, may we leave a lingering scent of His heavenly aroma. That all may know! Or at the very least begin to wonder.

The Banyan Tree

But now are they many members, yet but one body.
1 Corinthians 12:20

The banyan fig tree is one of the most massive trees in the world. One particular tree in India is more than five hundred and fifty years old and has a branch spread that covers about five acres. It looks more like a grove of trees than a single tree, but it is a single tree connected to a sole source.

Some unique features of the banyan tree allow it to grow large and last longer than most other trees. Consider a comparison of how the church has the potential to be like the banyan tree in growth and stability. And Christ boldly proclaimed of His church: "... the gates of hell shall not prevail against it" (Matthew 16:18).

In an effort to fulfill the great commission, the church I pastor started extensions in surrounding communities. Starting one such church proved to be a roller-coaster-ride of victories and disappointments, and we almost gave up. But we proceeded with the promise of Christ, "I am with you alway, even unto the end of the world" (Matthew 28:20). We began by holding services in a motel conference room, but due to the early Sunday morning singing (sometimes before residents had awakened), the proprietor soon stopped renting to us. Our search continued, and our pastor for this outreach, Jon Mains, found a wonderful hall in which to conduct services at an unbelievably low cost of two hundred dollars a month. After the first year, without warning, the manager raised the rent to one thousand dollars a month. We felt it too expensive for the two-hour weekly service, so we searched for a more economical location. What a thrill when a local congregation allowed us to share their facilities! However, after only three services in what was actually a church building, the pastor of that church informed us that, due to their default on the mortgage, the building was going into a sheriff's sale on Thursday of the coming week. During the Sunday service at our primary church, we prayed for a miracle. And we were greatly encouraged by a dream Pastor Mains' wife, Rebekah, shared. In her dream, money rained from a blue sky, and as she lifted her open hands to receive the blessing, a set of keys fell from the sky into her hand.

The week began with some great news: a foundation in the area promised to redeem the property so it could continue to serve the churches. We went to the sheriff's sale to see this miracle unfold, but the foundation representative was running late. We pleaded with the sheriff to stall the sale until the foundation representative arrived with a check to redeem the property. He asked if anyone objected to waiting five more minutes, and explained, "I'm told a person with a check to redeem the property should be walking through the door any minute. Surely no one would object to us waiting for the property to be redeemed for the sake of two congregations who worship in the building." Sadly, one man did object, so the sale began. My heart sank. God, where are you in all of this, I wondered.

The Banyan Tree

The man who objected to the delay of the bidding made a bid reflecting the price of the unpaid mortgage. At that very moment, the foundation representative arrived and explained that he had a check for $160,000 to redeem the property. "Sorry, the sale has started," the sheriff explained. I felt like it was the end of our dreams, hopes, and prayers. If only God had been one minute earlier! I momentarily forgot that God is never late.

The congregation who owned the property did not make a bid, so I made a quick decision. Turning to the foundation director, I asked, "If I bid on the property and get the bid, can I have the check to help us purchase the property?" A man I'd never seen before said, "Yes." He gave us the check.

I turned to a friend who had come with me and expressed, "I will only bid up to one hundred seventy-five thousand. That will cost us fifteen thousand cash." The man bidding against me ran the bid to one hundred seventy-four thousand, five hundred dollars. My next bid was my limit, so in the most confident voice I could muster for one making his final bid, I exclaimed, "One hundred seventy-five thousand dollars." The other bidder dropped his gaze for a moment, looked up, and shook his head. We had won the bid!

Back to Rebekah's testimony of her dream: Money raining from the blue sky ... keys falling from the sky into her hand. Would you like to know the name of the foundation whose representative I had never before met, but who handed me a check for one hundred and sixty thousand dollars? The name of that foundation is Blue Sky Foundation!

We have often rejoiced over that miracle, but the greatest miracle of all is not the acquiring of the building; rather, the greatest miracle is the growing congregation who occupies the building. When we think of the word "church," we immediately get a mental picture of a building, and too often we place most of the emphasis upon the structure. And the church campus usually consumes most of our time and finances for upkeep and mortgage. I'm not suggesting we forsake our church buildings, but the real church—the church that God recognizes—is not the brick and mortar edifice. The actual church is the people who occupy the building and the people within the community whom we need to reach with the Gospel. That's where we need to focus most of our attention: building the congregation, which is the body of Christ.

Let's get back to the analogy of the banyan tree. It's features allow it to grow large and last longer than most. Consider a comparison of how the church has the potential to be like the banyan tree in growth.

"But now are they many members, yet but one body" (1 Corinthians 12:20). This Scripture describes the church congregation. It starts small but grows far-reaching. When we consider the banyan tree as our analogy, we recognize our need for a source outside ourselves; we are connected to someone else: Jesus Christ. The tree generally germinates in the crevice of another tree. It initially depends on life from another source. Ironically, considering the process of germination, most seeds of the banyan tree that fall onto the soil do not survive.

The Banyan Tree

First and foremost the church has its roots in Christ. The church is not the ingenuity of man. Second, I'm thinking of new converts in Christ. These "babes in Christ" need a source of strength from the family of believers. They are not designed to mature without the assistance of the body of believers. They may even need a specific person that comes into their lives to help them until they develop enough spiritual strength to take root on their own. Don't underestimate the worth and potential of a new believer, no matter how unlike the church they may appear. Give them time for growth. Until they mature, the church is an incubator for the weak, a hospital for the wounded, a school to train, inspiration for the weary, and hope for the helpless. "Till we all come in the unity of the faith, and of the knowledge of the Son of God, unto a perfect man, unto the measure of the stature of the fulness of Christ" (Ephesians 4:13).

Once the banyan sapling—that has germinated in the crevice of another tree—has gained some measure of maturity, a sprout grows down to the ground and puts roots into the soil. In time, this becomes the primary trunk of a banyan tree. Over time, the tree spreads outward to the point that its branches cannot support its weight, but something unique takes place that allows the tree to continue growing. The branches continue to put down roots into the soil, and each time this happens, the tree grows what is called an aerial prop root. Once this root matures, the prop root grows into an additional trunk that helps support—prop up—the tree. These support trunks allow the tree to continue to spread its canopy. However, no matter how many prop roots become support trunks, the supporting trunk is never an individual tree; rather, the supporting trunk is still connected either directly or indirectly to the main trunk, the primary source. We are all connected to Christ. "But speaking the truth in love, may grow up into him in all things, which is the head, even Christ" (Ephesians 4:15).

A church can spread no farther than its support trunks. These support trunks are individuals who fulfill the roles of the various ministries of the church. These roles include individuals with spiritual gifts, administrative gifts, evangelism gifts, caring gifts, teaching gifts, technology gifts, and the willingness to serve in various capacities: the list goes on and on. That is why it is critical that we each use our God-given talents for Christ's Kingdom. But of utmost importance, all must remain connected to the main trunk: the body of believers which we call the church. And the head of the church is Christ, and Christ has established leadership within the organization, and we submit ourselves to the authority of such leaders. Through this process, the church continues to expand. We stay connected to the body through personal devotion, prayer, the study of the Word, humility, fellowship with other believers, church attendance, and involvement in ministry.

Through nature, we can see the design for the church: a body of many believers all connected to a primary source. Further, even though we remain connected to the primary source, we are limited in how far and wide we can grow as a church. Our growth depends on whether or not we develop additional support trunks. Each time a prop root forms into a supporting trunk, the church can expand and reach farther. The words of Ronald Reagan are certainly applicable: "There is no limit to the amount of good you can do if you don't care who gets the credit."

The Banyan Tree

Numerous individuals in the first church are notable pillars for the roles they performed. Enough could not be said about Paul and his associates, who under extreme circumstances, did missionary work throughout the Roman Empire. They seldom stayed in a city more than a few days, but the nucleus of believers they left behind built some wonderful congregations and expanded Christ's Kingdom. Individuals lending their talents to the Lord made all the difference. Lydia used her wealth and influence to help build a church in her city, Philippi. She housed Paul and Silas, and though they had to flee the city, pillars such as Lydia caused the church to become one of the most noteworthy churches in the New Testament. While other congregations were embroiled in conflict, or were departing from the message of grace, the Philippians matured in Christ and became one of the few churches to support Paul financially. Barnabas used his gift as a peacemaker to introduce Paul to the church at Jerusalem, and to salvage young John Mark when Paul rejected him. Doctor Luke used his talent for more than medical purposes as he accompanied Paul on some of his journeys and recorded the history of the first church. Though key players passed off the scene, the church continued to grow, because other individuals dared to offer their talents to Christ's cause.

Where do you fit within the church? Are you daily connected to the primary source, Christ, through prayer and devotion? What pillar do you represent? Are those young in Christ able to lean upon you? What are your talents? Do you use them for the Lord on a regular basis? What is your calling? Are you connected to the body through involvement in some form of ministry? What areas of Christ's Kingdom will suffer if you fail to do your part? Something to really think about, and maybe it is something you should do something about. Starting today!

The Lord Always Has Another Move

And it was about the sixth hour, and there was a darkness over all the earth until the ninth hour. And the sun was darkened, and the veil of the temple was rent in the midst. And when Jesus had cried with a loud voice, he said, Father, into thy hands I commend my spirit: and having said thus, he gave up the ghost.

Luke 23:44-46

Checkmate is a term in chess indicating one player's king is under direct attack and cannot avoid being captured. Delivering checkmate is the ultimate goal in chess. The game ends as soon as one of the kings is checkmated, because checkmate leaves the other player with no legal moves. The game is so complex that once both players make their first move, there are as many as four hundred possible board setups. After the second turn there is the possibility of almost two-hundred thousand setups, and the odds increase with the third set of moves. Still, a king can be checkmated in two moves if not properly protected.

The story abounds of two men visiting an art gallery, studying an unusual painting of a man playing chess with the devil. The ear-to-ear grin on the devil expresses that he has the man cornered. The title of the painting, Checkmate, indicates that the game is over. The devil has won. His opponent has no more moves.

One of the men studying the painting is an international chess champion. As he stares at the chess board in the drawing, he suddenly steps back and announces: "It's wrong! We have to contact the artist. He has to rename the painting."

"Why?" asked his friend.

"Because it's not checkmate. The king has another move."

At Golgotha the devil stood on the sidelines coaching the game of the ages. He had perfectly orchestrated this final move, and it seemed he would win. The reigning government, the dominant religion, and the masses of people all cheered in his favor. He heard the final cry, "It is finished." He saw the head of Christ slump to his chest and his body fall limp onto the weight of the nails. With fists stabbing skyward he proclaimed, "Checkmate! The King has no more moves." This seemed correct to those observing.

But Satan had sidestepped the eternal record of our Lord, and he jumped too soon to a conclusion, for God always has another move. Here's but one biblical example of many:

> A long time ago, in a far-away land, there lived a king, Ahasuerus, who wanted to select a queen. He searched far and wide for the right person to be his wife and be the queen of his kingdom. He found

The Lord Always Has Another Move

a young lady named Esther who pleased him very much. He married her, and she moved into the palace. But he did not know that she was of the people called "the Jews." And neither did he know that she served the one true God, called by multiple descriptive names, one being *El Shaddai*: Lord God Almighty, the all sufficient one.

Queen Esther's parents had died when she was a child, and her cousin, Mordecai, along with his wife, took her into their home and cared for her like their own daughter. Mordecai was a very religious person, and he also served the one true God of the Old Testament.

In the palace, many workers served Queen Esther, and she was an important person. But Mordecai visited her and reminded her that she must never forget that God had a special work for her to do that was more important than being queen.

Meanwhile, King Ahasuerus had a man who worked for him whose name was Haman. Not only was Haman narcissistic, he was extremely evil. He liked to be important, and he liked it when others were not. He craved to have people bow down to him, and plotted to that cause. One day he became very angry at Mordecai because he did not bow down and worship him. But Mordecai served only the God of Scripture, so he refused to bow in worship to a mortal. Haman got so irate that he schemed to kill Mordecai and all the people who served the God that Mordecai served. So, Haman went before the king and tricked him into signing a law that said on a certain day, all the people in his kingdom who served the God of Mordecai, would be killed. Queen Esther did not know about this wicked plan, so Mordecai went to see her and told her what she must do. She must inform the king that Haman's plan would cause her, and the people she loved, to be killed.

Esther pleaded their cause to King Ahasuerus. But the king explained to Esther, "As king of Persia, whenever I make a law, it cannot be rescinded; therefore, it must be obeyed." He could not take back the law he had so foolishly signed, even though it would cause Queen Esther, her relatives, and many of her friends to be killed.

It looked like there was no hope for Esther and her people. "Checkmate," the adversary exclaimed. But the king said, "Though I can't undo my previous action, I still have other decrees I can make." And he wrote another law that said: "The people of Queen Esther have the right to defend themselves." Another move! So, the king sent riders on his fastest horses throughout his kingdom, and the couriers read the new law to all the people. Esther's people were not

The Lord Always Has Another Move

killed, for they were able to defend themselves from any enemy who attacked them. Instead of a Jewish bloodbath, many of their friends who did not serve the one true God helped to protect them from those who tried to harm them.

This story reveals some spiritual lessons:
- Even though we live for the Lord, life will still have its hardships.
- Even with the Lord on our side, there is still a great deal of effort that we must make to overcome the trials of life.
- Living for the Lord could well bring us extra trials, for the adversary hates God and delights in bringing harm to God's people.
- If you live for the Lord, you are a unique person, for the Lord always has another move for those who serve Him.

It looked like it was over for Moses and the Israelites when they came to the Red Sea. "Checkmate," Pharaoh proclaimed, as his chariots came upon the scared Israelites, crowding the shores of the daunting sea. But God always has another move: this time through the water instead of across the water.

The Israelite soldiers' knees knocked together when the Philistines sent out Goliath. "Send me a man!" his voiced boomed across the valley. Someone ran to king Saul and explained, "It's checkmate, sir. We're beaten." But God had another move already planned. It wasn't a bigger giant to face Goliath, not a better weapon, nor a stronger army. It was a young lad with a slingshot and five smooth stones he had selected from the creek bed. He had the Lord on his side, and his Lord knew of the one, unprotected and vulnerable spot on Goliath's body: his forehead. David took that move, and Goliath took his final move when he tumbled to the ground.

As the soldiers cast Daniel into the den of lions, his enemies high-fived each other and shouted, "Checkmate." But Daniel knew the Lord always had another move! He didn't necessarily know what that move would be, but he had seen the Lord at the chessboard before, and he knew, God always has the final say.

It was a game to the finish. Satan chasing Christ across the board of life:

- It began at his birth. Herod deceitfully requested of the three wise men: "And when ye have found him, bring me word again, that I may come and worship him also" (Matthew 2:8). As the wise men left the room, Herod winked at the captain of his guard, and with a hideous smile proclaimed: "Checkmate." But the Lord always has another move! When necessary He dispatches angels to rescue. He sometimes demands demons to flee. At other times He commands nature to stand still. This time He had Joseph leave his country and journey back to the land of the former captivity of his people: Egypt. The land of former slavery gave him liberty to raise his son apart from fear of Herod's rage. How ironic is that!

The Lord Always Has Another Move

- For three years of ministry, Christ always had another move. Over disease. Over demons. Over death. In a single chapter of the Bible (Mark 5), Christ showed His authority over mankind's worst enemies: demons, disease, and death—Legions at Gadara; the woman with a blood disease; a damsel raised from the dead.
- As the events of Calvary unfolded, it looked like the end: "It is finished," Jesus said. "Checkmate!" Satan proclaimed. Demons rejoiced. Distraught friends placed Jesus' body inside a borrowed tomb. But even the devil seemed a little nervous, so the tomb was sealed and soldiers were dispatched to guard it. But sometime between the Sabbath and Sunday morning, God decided to make His next move. For God always has another move!

The death of the Savior certainly looked like "checkmate" against the promised church. Contrary to Christ's promise, the "gates of hell" seemed to have prevailed. But they should have known better, for Lazarus was a member of their congregation. Even so, Sunday's headlines shattered hell's gates. And the resurrected Savior made another power-move, one the adversary had not anticipated: "And Jesus came and spake unto them, saying, All power is given unto me in heaven and in earth" (Matthew 28:18). But then He left them again. Alone, without the promised comforter.

For several days, the church huddled in an upper room, awaiting God's next move. They'd heard about the promised power, but none could fully comprehend what was about to happen. God had spoken in the Old Testament about a particular move: a move reserved for the right moment. "And it shall come to pass afterward, that I will pour out my Spirit upon all flesh..." (Joel 2:28)." To their amazement, God made that move during the Feast of Pentecost, the church's birth: "And suddenly there came a sound from heaven as of a rushing mighty wind, and it filled all the house where they were sitting. And there appeared unto them cloven tongues like as of fire, and it sat upon each of them. And they were all filled with the Holy Ghost, and began to speak with other tongues, as the Spirit gave them utterance" (Acts 2:2-4). The disciples were not sure what to expect: they simply were doing what He had told them to do just before He departed from them into heaven. "... tarry ye in the city of Jerusalem, until ye be endued with power from on high" (Luke 24:49). They did. And they saw their checkmate reversed by this never-before-used move of Christ: Holy Spirit infilling. The Holy Spirit entered them, emboldened them, and empowered them. They went from a disappointed and defeated group of followers to being a proactive group of leaders: all in a moment's experience of the Spirit infilling. Soon after, this group became accused of turning the world upside down (Acts 17:6).

Satan has tried many "checkmate" moves against the church. Confusion regarding biblical doctrines was an elaborate game-changer. Separate the godhead of Scripture into multiple persons instead of the Monotheistic God of Scripture. Have believers pray to saints instead of the Savior, and if that doesn't work, have them appeal to Christ's mother. Keep on baptizing, but eliminate the saving name: Jesus. Substitute the Holy Spirit infilling with sprinkling of water, or a picture of a dove, or some smoking incense:

The Lord Always Has Another Move

something other than the supernatural infilling of the Spirit. And so, the church lapsed into apostasy, seemingly to never recover. But that changed at the dawning of the twentieth century when the Holy Spirit descended upon a handful of seekers in Topeka, Kansas. And on to Azusa. And Europe. And to the uttermost parts of the earth. The Holy Spirit invasion continues to prevail across the land.

The worst of the curses of Adam's failure was death: "… thou shalt surely die" (Genesis 1:17). Since Adam and Eve's tragic decision, mankind has succumbed to death. Death seems a "checkmate" move. But even death is not the final move against Christ-followers: Christ gave us that assurance when He stood at the tomb of His friend and commanded, "… Lazarus, come forth," (John 11.43). Christ reserves that move for us: "Behold, I shew you a mystery; We shall not all sleep, but we shall all be changed, In a moment, in the twinkling of an eye, at the last trump" (1 Corinthians 15:51-52); "For the Lord himself shall descend from heaven with a shout … and the dead in Christ shall rise first: Then we which are alive and remain shall be caught up…. to meet the Lord in the air: and so shall we ever be with the Lord" (1 Thessalonians 4:16-17). What a power move that will be! And that is but the beginning of eternal bliss for the believers.

Where are you in this sermon? How do you apply its contents to your situation? Who, or what, is your Haman that is trying to destroy you? You need to take a trip into the King's throne-room. He's not just an earthly king, but He is the King of kings and Lord of lords! There's a huge difference in our King and the king in the story of Esther. King Ahasuerus did not know Esther's story; in contrast to our King, she had to tell him what was happening. She was not even sure how he would respond: he could have her killed for coming into the throne-room uninvited, or he could welcome her with his outstretched scepter. Our King already knows our need, and He has given us an open invitation into his throne-room. He is waiting for us to submit ourselves under His protection: "Let us therefore come boldly unto the throne of grace, that we may obtain mercy, and find grace to help in time of need" (Hebrews 4:16). No matter how bad the situation, stay in His presence, for our Lord will always have another move!

The devil's final move is recorded in Scripture: he moves into an eternal lake of fire (Revelation 20:10). Of course, this is not by choice; he is forced into that move. "Checkmate!" Christ will proclaim. But long after that, our Lord will still make moves. He moves us into a new heaven and a new earth (Revelation 21); He will begin eternity for us, where there is no more curse. How exciting to see that one of his last recorded moves in Scripture is the reversal of the Genesis curse (Genesis 3 versus Revelation 22). No more death. The tree of life, removed from the garden, will reclaim its place among God's redeemed. Indeed, our God is the Master of the game, always with another move.

What jam is your life in? What corner are you backed into? What impossible situation has captured your life. Look to the One Who commands tomorrow. Pray to the One Who knows no defeat. Submit to the One Who sees every situation. Call out to the One Who cares about your every dilemma. He has another move for you!

Monotheism

For God so loved the world, that he gave his only begotten Son, that whosoever believeth in him should not perish, but have everlasting life.

John 3:16

Take heed therefore unto yourselves, and to all the flock, over the which the Holy Ghost hath made you overseers, to feed the church of God, which he hath purchased with his own blood.

Acts 20:28

It is extremely important to understand Who saves us and how we are saved; further, we need to realize that our Savior desires a personal and intimate relationship with His children! While some religions stress appeasing the gods, the God of the Bible came to the earth with this sole purpose, "... to seek and to save that which was lost" (Luke 19:10).

Before Edwin Hubble, who died in 1953, astronomers thought the Milky Way galaxy in which we live was the only galaxy making up the universe. Now, with the invention of the Hubble Telescope, named in honor of Mr. Hubble, we realize our assumption of the size of the universe was way off. My cousin, Jeff Smiley, shared a remarkable story relating to this discovery. His son Will is a student at the Naval Academy in Annapolis, Maryland. On one of the family's visits to see Will, they met Jim Jeletic, who is second in command at the Hubble Space Telescope Project at NASA's Flight Center in Greenbelt, Maryland. Jeff asked Mr. Jeletic, "What is the most exciting thing that has happened in your work?"

Mr. Jeletic explained that they once observed a spot in outer space that you could cover by holding your thumb at arm's length and looking at it with one eye closed. In that small spot in outer space, in a ten day period, they discovered three thousand galaxies that were new to them. Sometime later, they used a higher caliber lens and observed another spot of similar size for eleven days. During this time they discovered another ten thousand galaxies.

We now realize there are as many as one-hundred billion galaxies—and counting. Scientists project there are as many as two-hundred billion galaxies that make up the universe. Our galaxy, the Milky Way, is one-hundred thousand light years across. A light year is the distance light can travel in a year: almost six trillion miles. Our galaxy is but one of perhaps two-hundred billion galaxies: incomprehensible to most, if not all of us. And as Christians we serve the creator of this vast universe. "In the beginning God created the heaven and the earth" (Genesis 1:1). This Creator is the one Who came and communed with Adam and Eve, removed Himself because of their sin, and is the One Who later came to earth to save us "with His own blood ..." This is the same God Who in Spirit form, indwells us today.

When I was young, I struggled knowing how to pray to this God. Because of the various scriptural terms for God, I would pray

Monotheism

to God the Father for a while, to the Holy Spirit for a while, and then to Jesus for a while. I was concerned I would make one of the others jealous. So, I would switch it up, but I always went back to Jesus, for I preferred Him because of Calvary.

This confusion of who God was did not exist in the beginning. Adam and Eve knew God as the Creator Who communed with them. After they sinned, they knew Him as the God Who judged them and cast them out of the Garden of Eden. In the Exodus wandering, one of the first concepts God reinforced was that the God of Judaism was only one God, and He is the only God: "Hear, O Israel: The Lord our God is one Lord" (Deuteronomy 6:4). This God went by multiple names in Scripture:
- (God) Elohim
- (Lord God Almighty) El Shaddai
- (Lord, Master) Adonai
- (Jehovah or Yahweh) translated LORD in the English Bible

Multiple names for God in the Old Testament do not represent multiple gods; they are merely descriptive names of the One and only God of creation. When Jesus was born, His name was not a random choice: angels specifically told Joseph and Mary what name to call Him. The English rendition, Jesus, means "Jehovah has become our salvation." God our Creator became our Savior through Christ. The prophet of old had proclaimed: "Therefore the Lord himself shall give you a sign; Behold, a virgin shall conceive, and bear a son, and shall call his name Immanuel" (Isaiah 7:14). Immanuel means "God with us."

There seemed to be no controversy about who God was in the first church. Coming from Judaism, when the early Christians accepted Christ, they recognized Him as God. And the name of Jesus proved dominant in the early church. Paul wrote regarding Christ:

> Let this mind be in you, which was also in Christ Jesus: Who, being in the form of God, thought it not robbery to be equal with God: But made himself of no reputation, and took upon him the form of a servant, and was made in the likeness of men: And being found in fashion as a man, he humbled himself, and became obedient unto death, even the death of the cross. Wherefore God also hath highly exalted him, and given him a name which is above every name: That at the name of Jesus every knee should bow, of things in heaven, and things in earth, and things under the earth; And that every tongue should confess that Jesus Christ is Lord, to the glory of God the Father.
>
> Philippians 2:5-11

Some quickly point out that this and other verses mention both the Father and the Son, so isn't that two different people? No, these terms describe One God in purpose, not persons, for He remains one God. He is God the Creator of life (Father). This same God, in Spirit form, " ... moved upon the face of the waters" (Genesis 1:2) in the beginning of the Old Testament. In the beginning of the New Testament this same Spirit overshadowed a virgin and caused her to miraculously conceive. That miraculous, human conception (Jesus) became the abode of the eternal Spirit of God, for God needed a body to become the human sacrifice to pay our debt of sin. Because

Monotheism

the death of animals could not suffice for the sins of humanity, God prepared Himself a body to die to pay mankind's debt of sin. "For the wages of sin is death; but the gift of God is eternal life through Jesus Christ our Lord" (Romans 6:23).

Jesus was not a second person in the Godhead Who took on human flesh; rather, the one eternal God of creation took on human flesh, and that human flesh was called the Son of God: called the son of man because he was human, conceived in the womb of the virgin Mary; likewise, He was called the Son of God because the Holy Spirit caused His conception in Mary's womb. The Apostle Paul explained, "… God was in Christ, reconciling the world unto himself…" (2 Corinthians 5:19).

We use the term God the Father in reference to God giving life to all mankind, including Jesus. And since God gave life to the man Jesus Christ, Jesus is referred to as God's Son instead of Joseph's son. Joseph's son could not save us, but the Son of God (God in human form) could save us. Though having lived a sinless life, Jesus died the death of a sinful man. And being God, He allowed His death to suffice for the sins of all who would accept His sacrifice.

The birth of Jesus was the first and only time God became a human. And being conceived of the Holy Spirit, the Scripture uses the terminology "the only begotten of the Father …" (John 1:14).

Throughout Scripture, you will see references to God as Father, as Son, and as Spirit, but these are to show the purpose of Deity among us, not to show another person of the Godhead. The Godhead is complete in Jesus, for "… in him dwelleth all the fulness of the Godhead bodily" (Colossians 2:9).

- As the Father, God created us. Though He goes by multiple names in the Scripture, He remains one God.
- As a man, God came to minister and to die for His creation. Likewise, He goes by multiple names: Son of God, Jesus (meaning Jehovah has become our salvation), Lord (master), Christ (the anointed of God), Immanuel (God with us).
- As the Holy Spirit, God came to indwell us. So, God is our Creator, our Redeemer, our Transformer, but He is still the singular God of Scripture.

Oh, happy day when I realized God is one, and if in prayer I address Him by His multiple names, I am not addressing various persons; instead, I am addressing the One God of Scripture. He is not three: He is one. Whether I pray to Jehovah, or the Holy Spirit, or Jesus, or God the Father, I am praying to the singular, indivisible, one and only true God of Scripture.

Over time, church doctrines divided the God of Scripture into persons. Some have described the Godhead as being like a corporate board, or a committee: multiple persons who make up one group. In doing this, I believe we lose a personal experience of the intimate love God has for us: a board or committee is too impersonal. We lack understanding of the Holy Spirit power resident within us: the God Who created two-hundred billion galaxies indwells us in Spirit form. This one God became a man and walked the dusty roads of Judea, preaching the good news of salvation. And He is the one

Monotheism

Who hung on a splintery cross to shed His blood for us. This one God dwells within us, and it is Him we worship, pray to, serve, and will someday be with forever. When we pray, we are not praying to them: we are praying to Him.

Over time, church dogmas added Mary and saints as intermediaries to God. So, many petition Christ's mother to get to the Son, to plead to the Father. Others ask a saint to intercede on their behalf. Doctrines of man push us farther away from a personal relationship with the singular God of creation. But we don't have to do so. For when we pray, we can pray to the one Who created us, the one Who became one of us at Bethlehem's birth, and paid our debt of sin at Calvary. This loving God purchased the church "with His own blood" (Acts 20:28). Our Father God could not have done this without a human body.

The prophet described the Incarnation: " For unto us a child is born, unto us a son is given: and the government shall be upon his shoulder: and his name shall be called Wonderful, Counsellor, The mighty God, The everlasting Father, The Prince of Peace" (Isaiah 9:6). God became a man in Christ Jesus.

In several Scriptures, the Bible gives credit to the God of the Old Testament and to Jesus of the New Testament as performing the same act or being the only one to possess a characteristic. Here are examples: both are called the creator of the world; both are called all-powerful; both are the first and the last; both are the Savior of mankind. How can both be all of these? Because they are one! Consider these verses:

He was in the world, and the world was made by him, and the world knew him not. He came unto his own, and his own received him not.

John 1:10-11

And without controversy great is the mystery of godliness: God was manifest in the flesh, justified in the Spirit, seen of angels, preached unto the Gentiles, believed on in the world, received up into glory.

1 Timothy 3:16

For by him were all things created, that are in heaven, and that are in earth, visible and invisible, whether they be thrones, or dominions, or principalities, or powers: all things were created by him, and for him. For in him dwelleth all the fulness of the Godhead bodily.

Colossians 1: 16; 2:9

And Jesus came and spake unto them, saying, All power is given unto me in heaven and in earth.

Matthew 28:18

How can the Scriptures justifiably say these things if the Godhead is multiple persons? If Jehovah is the first and last, how can Jesus be the first and the last? Because God is one, the Scripture can give all the characteristics of this singular God to any manifestation of God, whether as Creator, as Redeemer, or as Deliverer. Further, why in the New Testament is there so much emphasis on the name

Monotheism

of Jesus? In fact, Paul wrote: "And whatsoever ye do in word or deed, do all in the name of the Lord Jesus, giving thanks to God and the Father by him" (Colossians 3:17). Consider why the Scripture stresses the name of Jesus:

- In baptism: We are baptized into the name God chose for His role as redeemer. All were baptized in Jesus' name: Jewish converts, Acts 2:38; Samaritan converts, Acts 8:16; Gentile converts, Acts 10:48; disciples baptized by John were re-baptized, Acts 19:5. We identify with Christ's death through baptism into His name.
- In prayer: We are calling upon the name of the One Who—because He became a human and dwelt among us—understands our needs. As God, He is able to supply our needs. And Christ gave us directions for petitioning heaven: ask in His name: "If ye shall ask any thing in my name, I will do it" (John 14:14).
- In suffering: Jesus understands our pain because He suffered much, but He chose for His suffering not to be in vain. He applied His suffering to our credit, like a prepaid account from which we can withdraw in time of need. The prophet of old said it well when speaking of Christ: "Surely he hath borne our griefs, and carried our sorrows" (Isaiah 53:4).
- In worship: "For where two or three are gathered together in my name, there am I in the midst of them" (Matthew 18:20).

Over time, the Old Testament doctrine of monotheism became

distorted. The developing church purposefully divided the Godhead into two persons (the Father and the Son). The Ecclesia later determined the Holy Spirit was also a person. This particular doctrine of the Godhead determined there were three persons making up the Godhead, with separate personalities, separate responsibilities, and separate identities. So, the New Testament picture of the Godhead depicted by paintings and sculptures is generally three persons: an old man sitting on a throne (the Father); a baby cradled in the arms of a woman (the Son); a dove descending from the sky (the Holy Spirit).

Let's repaint this picture of the Godhead from the artists' perspective to a biblical description of God. First, let's white out the picture of an aged man depicting the Father, for the God of Genesis is an invisible Spirit Who dwells among some 200 billion galaxies. God doesn't sit on a throne somewhere in the universe, the universe exists in Him. Still, let's remember that He focused His love on the inhabitants of a little planet in the Milky Way called Earth. This invisible and all-powerful God robed Himself temporarily in a human-like form in the Old Testament to appear unto individuals such as Adam and Eve and Abraham. We call this a theophany: a visible, human-like manifestation of God. Generally, however, manifestations of God's presence in the Old Testament were inhuman: a wind, a fire, a cloud. He is a Spirit, and in Spirit form He is everywhere at all times. There is no place where you can go that He is not. The Holy Spirit is not a separate person in the Godhead; rather, the Holy Spirit is the monotheistic, invisible God manifesting His presence: sometimes in great power and sometimes in a manner that only those truly seeking Him can recognize. At the

Monotheism

descent of the Holy Spirit on the Day of Pentecost (the inauguration of the church), a rushing mighty wind and tongues of fire became perceptible. And the invisible God indwelt mankind.

Christ, the Son of God—conceived by the Holy Spirit—was the only human manifestation of God. We can only guess at what Christ may have looked like while He ministered on the Earth. But that image has certainly changed. For a more up-to-date picture of Christ, let's consider the scene that the Apostle John saw when he came face-to-face with Jesus some fifty plus years after the crucifixion:

> I was in the Spirit on the Lord's day, and heard behind me a great voice, as of a trumpet, Saying, I am Alpha and Omega, the first and the last: and, What thou seest, write in a book, and send it unto the seven churches which are in Asia; unto Ephesus, and unto Smyrna, and unto Pergamos, and unto Thyatira, and unto Sardis, and unto Philadelphia, and unto Laodicea. And I turned to see the voice that spake with me. And being turned, I saw seven golden candlesticks; And in the midst of the seven candlesticks one like unto the Son of man, clothed with a garment down to the foot, and girt about the paps with a golden girdle. His head and his hairs were white like wool, as white as snow; and his eyes were as a flame of fire; And his feet like unto fine brass, as if they burned in a furnace; and his voice as the sound of many waters. And he had in his right hand seven stars: and out of his mouth went a sharp twoedged sword: and his countenance was as the sun shineth in his strength. And

> when I saw him, I fell at his feet as dead. And he laid his right hand upon me, saying unto me, Fear not; I am the first and the last: I am he that liveth, and was dead; and, behold, I am alive for evermore, Amen; and have the keys of hell and of death.
>
> Revelation 1:10-18

The Apostle John had previously described the conversation of Pilate who prematurely proclaimed, "… behold the man" (John 19:5) in reference to Christ. But here John paints the image of the resurrected Christ. Though He had some human qualities, forget the image of a baby cradled in his mother's arms. Look upon the Divine, holding seven suns in His hand. See Him as the first and last. This is the God that has saved us, the God we serve, the God we worship, the God Who has entered into us, and the one and only God of Scripture. This God loved us so much that, though His features were as bright as the sun, He became mortal and allowed Himself to be crucified to pay our debt of sin so we can live with Him forever.

Why hesitate in accepting the Bible truth that Jesus is God? Couple that with the Bible proclamation that God is one. Further, if God is one, let's stop dividing Him into three separate persons, praying first to one and then the other. Let's recognize Him as the singular God of the universe, Who loves us very much and desires to have us in His fellowship for eternity.

The Story Of Dawson Springs

And the Lord shall guide thee continually, and satisfy thy soul in drought, and make fat thy bones: and thou shalt be like a watered garden, and like a spring of water, whose waters fail not.

Isaiah 58:11

The writer of the book of Hebrews alludes to a time when everything that can be shaken will be shaken: governments, the economy, religion, and relationships. In the last days perilous times (dangerous, unsafe, terrifying times) shall come, so says the Scripture (2 Timothy 3:1). But also, in the last days, the Scripture proclaims the Lord would pour out His Spirit upon the whole world. We can be affected adversely by the perilous times, but we can be enriched spiritually by the Holy Spirit outpouring!

Dawson, Kentucky, was one of the boomtowns of the latter eighteen and early nineteen hundreds. Washington Hamby, an ex-Confederate cavalryman who owned the Hamby Hotel, had dug a well and struck mineral water. It became advertised as medicinal waters, and folks came from hundreds of miles to drink and bathe in these healing waters. One advertisement read: "If you seek rest,

Come. If you are sick, Come. Drink of the life-giving waters and return home healed and rejuvenated." Sounds like promises from Scripture, and people bought into the hope. The town prospered:

- Forty hotels and boarding houses sprang up and catered to thousands of visitors annually.
- One hotel alone had five hundred rooms.
- Forty mineral wells were soon supplying the needs of the guests.
- In 1898, for emphasis, the city officials added "springs" to the name: making the town Dawson Springs.
- The Illinois Central Railroad sold over 50,000 tickets to Dawson Springs in a single year.
- The Pittsburgh Pirates baseball team moved their spring training camp to Dawson Springs and drank of the waters believed to make people healthy.
- The town built a professional baseball stadium with an indoor athletic building.
- The mineral water was bottled and shipped to various parts of the world, and fortunes were made.
- One of the finest hotels—a three-story building—had its own electric company, had a ballroom with its own orchestra, and it was magnificent even by today's standards.

Ironically, a century later, Dawson Springs has less than three thousand residents. Its hotels have long crumbled. There are no fancy restaurants and no malls. They don't even have a Walmart, and most shopping is done at a Dollar Store. Quite a downgrade

The Story Of Dawson Springs

from where they were in the early nineteen hundreds! How could a town reach such heights only to slip into such obscurity in a mere hundred years?

Part of the answer: It was built on deception, or at best, misinformation. The waters were not medicinal. In fact, they were not springs: they were shallow wells that eventually became exhausted by overuse. The town should have been named Dawson Wells. Today, few people know where Dawson Springs is located; fewer still visit. It is probably more known for a mailman, who a few years back, stashed 44,900 pieces of mail in his dead mother's house and in a rented storage unit, instead of delivering them to his customers.

I see a comparison of Dawson Springs and modern Christianity: too much of Christianity is mere shallow wells. Many are traditional wells that have grown stagnant, and some have completely dried up, even though the Lord has promised we can drink from a spring of water that never fails: "… but whoever drinks the water I give them will never thirst. Indeed, the water I give them will become in them a spring of water welling up to eternal life" (John 4:14 NIV). Too many congregations are built upon man-made traditions instead of scriptural truth. Yet, Jesus proclaimed that the church would be a vibrant entity, free of the stagnant dregs of traditionalism. "God is a Spirit: and they that worship him must worship him in spirit and in truth" (John 4:24).

Consider the uniqueness of a naturally flowing spring versus a well where man digs until he finds the water table:

- Wells sometime dry up; springs seldom run dry.
- Wells depend upon seasonal rain; the water from springs gushes from a deep reservoir, a greater source.
- Wells sometime stagnate; springs are ever flowing.
- Wells are not self-purifying, so, bugs and critters pollute; conversely, springs are ever-flowing, remaining continually fresh.

My grandparents lived in Appalachia Kentucky. Their source of water was a hand-dug well, but bugs and various critters with multiple legs lived on the surface of the water and the sides of the damp, stone-lined walls. But a fish also lived in the well, keeping the critter population at bay. Somehow, grandpa felt the fish living in the well was a good thing. I've often wondered, who cleaned up after the fish's droppings? I'd prefer a continually flowing spring any day. The flowing of the Spirit of God is likened to a well-spring "… springing up …" (John 4:14). The Scripture describes the Holy Spirit as pure, deep, refreshing, and ever flowing.

Jesus had a conversation with a Samaritan woman at a well believed to be dug by Jacob of the Old Testament. She basically said, "We have our well and our traditions, both which go back a long way." She pointed to the distant mountain and proclaimed, "That's our mountain, our temple, our religion." Jesus explained, a time is coming when neither this place nor Jerusalem will matter, and traditions will be shattered, for they run dry and cannot fulfill the need. "But whosoever drinketh of the water that I shall give him shall never thirst…" (John 4:14).

The Story Of Dawson Springs

Some seasons are tougher, leaving wells stagnant and sometimes dry, but springs produce fresh water even in the barren seasons. In a spiritual sense, life has its seasons and can get tough. It's times like this that we need the deep-flowing, refreshing faith, else circumstances can leave us feeling defeated, confused, or cynical. The Christian can't survive on a constant diet of what this world gives. Daily newscasts leave the soul empty. One person told me he spends a lot of time absorbed in government and politics, and he's becoming very negative, identifying with politicians and programs instead of Christ and scriptural promises. Conversely, we need the daily refreshing that the Holy Spirit supplies.

Paul cautioned young Timothy that circumstances would get bad instead of better. He admonished him to stir up the spiritual gift within. We need the spiritual flowing springs of living water. How do we stir up the living water? It's back to the basics:

- Daily prayer: The creation communicates with the Creator.
- Daily Bible reading: The Word refreshes the soul.
- Fellowship with believers: They encourage and challenge one to be better, to grow deeper, to climb higher.
- Church attendance: We learn, share, and become refocused for the journey.

Nothing will suffice for these spiritual, living waters. Spiritual disciplines remain the source of deep-flowing springs of living water. All else is susceptible to drought, pollution, disaster, and man-made shortfalls.

Here's a good place to talk about the Holy Spirit baptism. John the Baptist referenced Spirit baptism, and Christ dictated Spirit baptism as an essential part of the New Birth experience (John 3). The Spirit baptism inaugurated the birth of the church, and the converts to the first church received the Spirit baptism. The Holy Spirit baptism is not a mere acknowledgment of one's faith; rather, it is a literal experience of Christ coming to dwell within the believer. From this point, the believer's lifestyle exemplifies faith in action. The Holy Spirit infilling is a supernatural baptism in God's presence that is evidenced by speaking in a language unknown by the individual recipient: Acts 2 (Jews), Acts 8 (Samaritans), Acts 10 (Gentiles), and Acts 19 (disciples of John). If at Spirit baptism the Jews spoke in tongues, and the Samaritans spoke in tongues (The Scripture doesn't specifically use these words regarding the Samaritans, but something so phenomenal happened that Simon tried to buy the ability to give the Holy Spirit to others.), and the Gentiles spoke in tongues, and the disciples of John the Baptist spoke in tongues when converting to Christianity, shouldn't believers today also speak in tongues when they receive the Holy Spirit?

Sad to say, many settle for tradition and don't seek the abundance of God's promises. Others accept whatever circumstances dictate. Like the king of old, when the golden shields representing honor were stolen, he settled for an inferior option: shields of brass (2 Chronicles 12:9-10). No matter how much you polish the surface, brazen shields can never suffice for golden ones. And no emblem, no ritual, and no tradition can suffice for the Holy Spirit baptism. All else are mere wells; conversely, Spirit baptism is living springs, ever fresh and overflowing.

The Story Of Dawson Springs

Sadly, many a soul who has settled for less, or has purposefully sought the shortcut in their Christian experience, has diminished into spiritual obscurity, just like Dawson Springs of old. However, when the world has lost hope and is wandering in the dry and barren desert of emptiness and meaninglessness, the Spirit-filled believer drinks from the ever-flowing springs of life. The Scripture promises: "And the Lord shall guide thee continually, and satisfy thy soul in drought, and make fat thy bones: and thou shalt be like a watered garden, and like a spring of water, whose waters fail not" (Isaiah 58:11).

So, where does one start? How about by asking the same question Paul asked the disciples of John the Baptist: "... Have ye received the Holy Ghost since ye believed?" (Acts 19:2). The Holy Spirit baptism is the fountain of life that Jesus referred to for future believers: "He that believeth on me, as the scripture hath said, out of his belly shall flow rivers of living water" (John 7:38). This is the experience of the believers at the birth of the church:

> And when the day of Pentecost was fully come, they were all with one accord in one place. And suddenly there came a sound from heaven as of a rushing mighty wind, and it filled all the house where they were sitting. And there appeared unto them cloven tongues like as of fire, and it sat upon each of them. And they were all filled with the Holy Ghost, and began to speak with other tongues, as the Spirit gave them utterance.
>
> Acts 2:1-4

There was a universal and uniform evidence of being filled with the Spirit: all of the one-hundred and twenty believers gathered in the upper room were baptized with the Spirit. All spoke in tongues. They spoke in a language they had not learned but were able to speak when the Spirit came into them and took control of that "unruly and evil" member of the body: the tongue (James 3:8). God, Who knows all languages, reversed the curse of Babel (Genesis 11). He allowed the believers to speak in a tongue unknown to them but known to witnesses of this supernatural event. When you are filled with the Holy Spirit, you, too, will experience this supernatural gift. This is not to discredit any experience you may have had in God; rather, it is to challenge all believers to not settle for anything less than this ever-flowing river of life.

Once filled with the Holy Spirit, the believer must learn to walk in the Spirit. The carnal man, like a tree cut off at the base, has a way of sprouting growth that, if unattended to, can smother the Spirit. Just as one eats three times daily to maintain proper health, the Spirit-filled man must partake of the things of God to maintain proper spiritual health: daily prayer, Bible reading, and fellowship with those who facilitate spiritual growth.

For too many, the Spirit baptism is a once-in-a-lifetime experience. Over time, they disconnect with the source of this living water Jesus spoke of to the Samaritan woman: "Jesus answered and said unto her, If thou knewest the gift of God, and who it is that saith to thee, Give me to drink; thou wouldest have asked of him, and he would have given thee living water" (John 4:10). Our children have a better grasp of this concept than some adults. They return from summer church camp all inspired about living for God, often

The Story Of Dawson Springs

with this testimony: "I received the Holy Ghost." "But I thought you already had received the Holy Ghost," we reply. "I got it again," they say, smiling from ear to ear. We, too, need renewed. Often. "And be not conformed to this world: but be ye transformed by the renewing of your mind, that ye may prove what is that good, and acceptable, and perfect, will of God." (Romans 12:2).

How can we be renewed in the Holy Spirit? It's simply a matter of returning with an open and seeking heart to the source of eternal life. "And ye shall seek me, and find me, when ye shall search for me with all your heart" (Jeremiah 29:13).

The Zeal Of The Lord

When we operate zealously, we put our whole heart, our time, our energy, and our finances into a project. We sometimes place other responsibilities on hold while we focus upon this single project that has consumed us. Often it is our zeal rather than expertise and resources that accomplish a task.

Zeal can have a negative connotation. Sometimes we equate zeal with being youthful or maybe a little foolish. And many times we operate out of enthusiasm but lack the wisdom that comes through the process of experience. Such mode of operation often fails and creates discouragement and frustration. Still, zeal is an essential quality for success in most every endeavor.

Zeal defined: enthusiasm, passion, fervor, intensity, urgency, having great value, determined. Zeal is a characteristic of God; thus, it became a characteristic of man when He created us "in His image" and "after His likeness," (Genesis 5:3). God was enthusiastic about His creation, and that is why the earth and all the universe is magnificent. Likewise, God desires zealousness from His creation toward Him. "If these hold their peace the very rocks will cry out," Jesus responded when someone tried to squash the zeal of worship toward Him. Further, God said to the lukewarm church in Revelation, "… be zealous therefore, and repent" (Revelation 3:19).

And the penalty for not doing so? "I will spew you out of my mouth" (Revelation 3:16).

Since zeal is innate, an endowed characteristic given to us by our Creator, we should take note of what God is zealous about. Further, we should attempt to emulate the same. The Bible speaks of three occasions regarding the zeal of the Lord.

The first occasion of the zeal of the Lord is mentioned in three places of Scripture: (2 Kings 19; 2 Chronicles 32; Isaiah 37). These Scriptures have to do with God delivering His people from their adversary.

A second occasion of the zeal of the Lord is the message of the Incarnation and the bringing about of humanity's redemption: God becoming man for the sake of dying for our sins. Isaiah prophesied, "Behold a virgin shall conceive and be with child…" (Isa 9:7). The question of "How could this impossible event transpire?" fell from the lips of all that searched the Scripture. The answer was within this proclamation: "The zeal of the Lord shall perform it."

The third occasion of the zeal of the Lord is when Christ went into the Temple at Jerusalem and turned over the tables of moneychangers, chasing out those that sold inferior sacrificial animals for an exorbitant price. Such unusual action set aback His disciples. They had never seen Christ display such emotion. "What's going on?" they questioned. Then they remembered the prophecy of old: "The zeal of thine house hath eaten me up" (Psalm 69:9; John 2:13-17).

The Zeal Of The Lord

Let's consider each of these three occasions where the zeal of God was the primary factor:

God's Zeal to Deliver His People

The first focus of God's zeal is on the deliverance of God's people from their adversary. Here's the story:

The time is the 700s BC. Sennacherib, King of Assyria, marched throughout his empire putting down rebellions, which included the Kingdom of Judah under the leadership of King Hezekiah. The Assyrians had devastated the ten northern tribes of Israel about thirty years before this event, but God had spared Judah and Jerusalem. With other nations rebelling against Assyria's demands of tribute, Hezekiah, likewise, followed suit. Sennacherib marched his army to the walls of Jerusalem, surrounded the city (cutting off any attempt of escape) and sent his charismatic ambassador, Rabshakeh, to demand Judah's surrender. Rabshakeh deliberately spoke in the Hebrew language regarding the demands of King Sennacherib, making sure the ordinary soldiers on the wall could understand his threats. He made accusations against Judah's trust in Egypt to deliver them. He reiterated the Assyrian victories over other nations and cities. He challenged them as to why they thought a small and isolated Judah could escape his mighty war-machine.

Hezekiah's actions showed the desperate situation but also his faith in the God of Judah. Instead of mounting the wall with a rebuttal, he went to the Temple, and there he petitioned the Lord.

Hezekiah's representatives pleaded for Rabshakeh to speak to them in the Assyrian tongue. They feared the threats would spread fear throughout the city and that panic would defeat the people before the battle started. But Rabshakeh continued to speak in the Hebrew language and even mocked them in their native tongue. And true to Hezekiah's concerns, fear gripped the people's hearts.

But then Rabshakeh made a fatal mistake: he challenged whether or not Judah's God was able to deliver them. After all, no other god had been able to stop this mighty army who believed their god had given them victory over all the other cities and nations that had rebelled against them. That was a mistake, for the one true God in heaven heard these accusations and this challenge, and a fiery resistance arose inside Him. First, He sent the prophet Isaiah to give Hezekiah and all Judah a message of hope:

> And Isaiah said unto them, Thus shall ye say unto your master, Thus saith the Lord, Be not afraid of the words that thou hast heard, wherewith the servants of the king of Assyria have blasphemed me. Behold, I will send a blast upon him, and he shall hear a rumour, and return to his own land; and I will cause him to fall by the sword in his own land.
>
> Isaiah 37:6-7

Second, that night God sent an angel of death throughout the camp of Assyria, and 185,000 men died. The remainder returned home, where two of Sennacherib's sons assassinated him.

The Zeal Of The Lord

Third, God's provisions didn't stop with the defeat of Judah's enemy one time. God proclaimed, not only have I delivered Judah, but I will continue to deliver them. Though intermittently punished for sins and eventually dispersed throughout the world, after some 1900 years of modern disbursement, God returned the Israelites to their homeland. And during the tribulation period, when Israel will be surrounded by the nations of the world who are bent on destroying them, God has promised that He will spare a remnant. Unheard of before! How can this be? "… the zeal of the Lord of hosts shall do this" (Isaiah 37:32).

Finally, though this promise was made directly to God's people, Judah, the concept remains true for God's people of all time. God's zeal motivates Him to fight for His own. Still today! Do you have an enemy attacking you? Is some sin trying to return into your life? Are the pleasures of the world beckoning you? Is Satan giving you a hard time? There is nothing that stirs the heart of God more than the enemy attacking His own. What you need to do, like Hezekiah of old, is bring your battles to the Lord, where His zeal motivates Him to fight for you. Find an altar and repent for any infraction against the Lord (2 Chronicles 7:13-14; Jeremiah 18:8, 26:3,13). Further, plead your case with God. When His fiery indignation is stirred, nothing can stand against Him.

Give God praise before and after He answers your request. Miriam, the sister of Moses, along with other devout women of the Exodus, danced to the beat of tambourines in praising God for His victorious performance at the Red Sea. But there should have been two acts to this drama of praise: one on both sides of the sea.

God's Zeal for the Incarnation

A second occasion of the Zeal of the Lord is the message of the Incarnation and the bringing about of man's redemption: God becoming man for the sake of dying for humanity's sins. Isaiah prophesied, "Behold a virgin shall conceive and be with child …" (Isaiah 9:7). How could the impossible happen? How can a child be conceived without the necessary process for conception? How is this going to happen? The answer: "The zeal of the Lord of hosts will perform this."

And so, God dispatched an angel to earth to commune with a young virgin named Mary, to ask her permission to participate in this miracle. She consented, and in a moment, He who had no beginning nor ending, the great "I Am" of Scripture, the Self-sufficient One from eternity, the One Who derives His existence from no one else, stepped from the realm of His everlasting Majesty and condescended into an embryonic stage of beginning. And the maker and controller of the seas floated in the amniotic fluid of total dependence.

Likewise, the zeal of the Lord sent the angel to the man engaged to Mary, Joseph, to explain what was happening. Most men, if not all, would have refused to accept such a far-fetched story, but the zeal of the Lord remained the convincing force. Joseph accepted the responsibility to participate in mankind's redemption.

Nine months later, Mary wrapped her baby in swaddling clothes, laid Him in a feeding trough, and lovingly stared into the eyes of the star-maker. Never before had an angelic choir took earth's stage.

The Zeal Of The Lord

Lowly shepherds received the first invitation to gaze upon the God-child. Wise men from afar, entirely out of touch with the current events surrounding Judea, came bearing gifts to an unknown King. The prophet foretold that He would be called Immanuel, God with us. The angel announced His name: Jesus—Jehovah has become our salvation. So began a thirty-three-year plan for the redemption of humankind, though the plan was as old as the earth itself: "… the Lamb slain from the foundation of the world" (Revelation 13:8).

No sooner had this miraculous birth of Christ taken place than Satan devised a plan to steal the miracle. The depraved king and arch-enemy of truth, Herod, sent soldiers wielding swords to kill all male infants two years old and under in Bethlehem. "… In Rama was there a voice heard, lamentation, and weeping, and great mourning, Rachel weeping for her children …" (Matthew 2:18). Herod had killed before: his own children whom he viewed as a threat to his throne. So this seemed a minor occasion that Herod would nip in the bud. But this occasion was different than others, for the zeal of the Lord of hosts had performed the birth of this child. Don't anyone mess with the Lord when He is zealous about something! The zeal of the Lord gets heaven involved.

An angel of the Lord directed Mary and Joseph to take the child and flee into Egypt. Later, an angel directed them to go back to Israel.

Lingering in the shadow of every miracle is the miracle thief, but, like Mary and Joseph of old, you must cling tightly to your miracle and do your part to allow God's will to reign. Mary and Joseph endured the gossip, accepted relocation in a foreign land, traveled about 410 miles (part of the time heavy with child and part of the time carrying the child in her arms) from Nazareth to Bethlehem, from Bethlehem to Egypt—perhaps all the way to Alexandria—before they traveled another 410 miles from Egypt back home to Nazareth: possibly most of the time on foot. It has been estimated—considering Christ's ministry and Mary following Him some of the time—that Mary journeyed over 12,000 miles with Jesus by the time of His crucifixion. That's halfway around the world at the equator: around 500 days of walking. You have got to remain committed to your miracle, and the zeal of the Lord will fight for you. In so doing, your promised deliverance will come. It's not always enough to receive a miracle promise; you've got to cradle your miracle in your arms, look the enemy in the eye, and proclaim, "You can't have my baby—my miracle!"

After Jesus fasted for forty days, the adversary came to steal Christ's purpose. Sometime around His thirty-third birthday, the adversary showed up again, this time with the religious leaders and the government on his side. They arrested Christ and nailed Him Roman-style-crucifixion to a cross, where they mocked and humiliated Him. They drained the life from Him for six hours. The supposed Incarnation lay lifeless in a borrowed tomb. Both the miracle birth and Incarnation seemed meaningless at this point. The future felt hopeless, the miracle had faded, and the plan of redemption seemed thwarted. In between Calvary and the resurrection, probably no human soul other than Mary had any confidence the supposed Savior of the world could save them, but they all had failed to factor in the most significant point: the zeal of the Lord of host!

The Zeal Of The Lord

And so the Creator and Sustainer of the universe restrained Himself, waiting for the proper time to elapse, and when the alarm clock sounded, the eternal breath of the Creator entered into the corpse of Christ. No grave could hold Him, no stone doorway could prevent Him, no armed guards could halt Him, no enemy could conquer Him, and no force could equal His source of energy. That source? The zeal of the Lord!

Until the long, dark and chilly night of despair passes, you must cling to your miracle! How? Like Jesus, proclaim, "It is written!" If Jesus said it, believe it. Cling to the horns of the altar until God comes to your rescue. The zeal of the Lord of host will bring deliverance if you hang on.

Are we going to make it to heaven? God is more zealous about this than we can imagine: so devoted to this cause that He came as a man to pay a debt of sin He never made. His primary concern is our salvation. His zeal will get us there if we dare allow Him.

God's Zeal for Revival in His House

The Gospel of John reveals the third occasion of the zeal of the Lord.

> And the Jews' passover was at hand, and Jesus went up to Jerusalem, and found in the temple those that sold oxen and sheep and doves, and the changers of money sitting: and when he had made a scourge of small cords, he drove them all out of the temple, and the sheep, and the oxen; and poured out the changers'

money, and overthrew the tables; and said unto them that sold doves, Take these things hence; make not my Father's house an house of merchandise. And his disciples remembered that it was written, The zeal of thine house hath eaten me up.

John 2:13-17

The above Scriptures are the fulfillment of the Psalmist's prophecy: "For the zeal of thine house hath eaten me up; and the reproaches of them that reproached thee are fallen upon me" (Psalm 69:9). In a fury, Christ drives away the commercialism and greed that had invaded the Temple, proclaiming that it was a house of prayer, not a warehouse for profit. Interestingly, no one stopped Him. Almost everyone disapproved of what he did, but no one dared do anything about it. I believe this account has a host of lessons we could consider:

- Relish the opportunity of coming to church for prayer and worship.
- Realize the respect we should have for the church building and the reverence we should have for the God of the building.
- Recognize the importance of taking care of the church building. Parishioners should use their talents to keep the church in proper repair.

Personally, I love going to church, participating in worship, listening to an inspiring sermon, and feeling Christ's presence. Still, it is significant that after the Romans destroyed the Jewish temple in Jerusalem in 70 AD, God does not seem too concerned about

The Zeal Of The Lord

rushing to rebuild the temple. Why? God's greatest interest is not the building, but rather what takes place inside the temple. And let us define the temple of interest for the church: "What? know ye not that your body is the temple of the Holy Ghost which is in you, which ye have of God, and ye are not your own?" (1 Corinthians 6:19). And a primary event of the temple: "… my house shall be called a house of prayer." God is concerned that, more so than anything else, an attitude of prayer prevails within the church, for prayer unleashes the power of the Lord among us. Likewise, a lack of prayer makes for a ho-hum attitude: both in the pew and the pulpit.

Jesus was known specifically for His spiritual powers: casting out demons, healing the sick, raising the dead—all with His spoken word. Only once in Scripture did Jesus use physical force; ironically, this event was not about saving the world. Instead, His physical actions were against the hypocritical religious leaders. Jesus called the temple, not a house of prayer, but "a den of thieves." Hopefully, our churches are not indicative of the attitude that prevailed in the temple at Jerusalem during Christ's ministry. Still, the question needs to be asked of us today: What does Christ call our church—a house of talent, a house of fellowship, a house of clicks, a house of gossip, a house of intellect, a house of carnality? Hopefully, He calls it a house of prayer.

Strangely, we spend multiple millions of dollars to erect beautiful church buildings while Jesus' greatest commission to us often goes ignored: preach and teach the gospel to all the world. At the least, our missions giving should reflect our expensive church buildings. Our responsibility to the poor should resonate among us as we relish our comfy pews. Money assigned for outreach should be considered as significant as money designated for repairs. The greater the income, the greater the outflow to reach the lost. What most concerns God is not the cost of the building; instead, God is concerned about what is going on inside the building. In seventy years of New Testament history, there is not one reference to the church owning a church building; instead, they gathered in homes to break bread, they ministered in established synagogues and preached on street corners, they performed miracles at the gate of the temple, they waxed boldly from a desert pulpit, and they worshiped on the inside of prison bars. Why? Paul answered this question in his letter to the church family at Corinth. "Know ye not that ye are the temple of God, and that the Spirit of God dwelleth in you? If any man defile the temple of God, him shall God destroy; for the temple of God is holy, which temple ye are" (1 Corinthians 3:16-17). God is most concerned about what is happening within us, not about the conditions of our facilities. This is not to suggest we should neglect our church facilities; instead, I wish to draw emphasis to our primary purpose: "Go ye into all the world ..." (Mark 16:15).

We oft-times feel insignificant, unqualified, ill-equipped, and even helpless to grow the family of believers. But the burden of accomplishment does not rest upon us. The promised revival of Joel did not happen in the temple: it started in a second-floor, rented room. The end-time revival will not come through our talent; neither is it about our intellect and awesome sermons. It is whether or not we make God's house what it should be: a house of prayer. If we obey, pray, and believe, the zeal of the Lord will perform this!

The Zeal Of The Lord

Attending church is much more than a ritual. It is an event with a promise of God. Jesus proclaimed, "For where two or three are gathered together in my name, there am I in the midst of them." (Matthew 18:20). He is zealous regarding what happens in our lives every time we gather in His house. We, too, should be zealous. Like the psalmist of old, our attitude should reflect the significance of God's house. The psalmist expressed an acceptable attitude about church attendance: "I was glad when they said unto me, Let us go into the house of the Lord" (Psalm 122:1). The church house should be one of our favorite places. The Psalms reinforce the importance of attending church, where God promises to meet us. "For a day in thy courts is better than a thousand. I had rather be a doorkeeper in the house of my God, than to dwell in the tents of wickedness" (Psalm 84:10).

When we attend church, we should not wait for things to happen; rather, we should instigate an atmosphere of worship unto God. "Enter into his gates with thanksgiving, and into his courts with praise: be thankful unto him, and bless his name" (Psalm 100:4). We should come with lofty expectations. Expect miracles. Believe for an outpouring of the Holy Spirit. Pray fervently for the lost to be saved. And if we do these things, in spite of the varying day-to-day circumstances that can frustrate the work of God, the zeal of the Lord will see to it that revival happens in our church.

There Will Come A Day

> Now there was a day when the sons of God came to present themselves before the Lord, and Satan came also among them.
>
> Job 1:1

Let's focus on the first five words of this Scripture: "Now there was a day ... ."

No matter who we are, how close to the Lord we live, or how well we plan our lives, there will come a day when the adversary plots against us. Satan's attacks take on many forms: a false accusation, an affliction, a temptation, a deception, or an all-out attack to destroy everything we are and have. And no matter how well we plan our lives, "there will come a day" of grave adversity.

I am aware that to compare our lives with Job may overwhelm some, especially when we consider all that he went through at the hand of Satan. We're quick to reflect, as good a man as Job was, if he could barely endure, then what chances have we of surviving an all-out attack from the adversary? We actually have a better chance of survival, for Job's test was a once-in-a-lifetime scenario. Yet, for all of us, maybe not today, and maybe not this year, there will come a day when we will have our faith tried. We will be challenged by the adversary, or circumstances, or by the adverse effect of some poor choices we make.

There came a day when dark and ominous clouds interrupted Job's routine, and in a matter of minutes, one after the other, four servants came running down the path that led to his front door to give him the heart-rending news that he had lost everything— including his children. All this in a single day: everything was lost except his wife.

Job's response to such tragedy defies human rational: "Then Job arose, and rent his mantle, and shaved his head, and fell down upon the ground, and worshipped" (Job 1:20). Worship the God who allowed this to happen? That's right. And what an incredibly positive example for us when our day of adversity comes! His response was not a reaction, for he was accustomed to daily prayer. His response was proactive. And this action is exactly what we need to do: bow our hearts and worship God. It is both an act of submission and an act of faith. These are not the responses the adversary expects; conversely, the normal human response is to question God's love. The adversary doesn't understand these responses of submission and faith from the believer toward his God; therefore, he has no weapon to counteract such, so he can't defeat us. Job survived the day. And the good news? We can also.

We say, "But I am not Job." We assume he was some superhero who had an unparalleled relationship with God. His strong faith and positive responses can make us feel insignificant. Actually, Job's life should be an encouragement to us, for he survived his tragedy with few of the spiritual resources we have. He had no Bible, no Holy

There Will Come A Day

Spirit indwelling, no church family, and he was a direct target of Satan for which he had no previous reference of defense. He was without a Bible, for he lived before the Scripture was written. He did not have the Holy Spirit baptism, for it wasn't yet given. He did not have a support system, for he was generally the one helping others in need. Even his closest friends judged him as having displeased God. And God had temporarily removed His hand of blessing to prove a point to Satan. But Job's response is exemplary: he bowed his heart and worshiped. Still, the drama continued. The Lord seemed silent long into Job's suffering. And when He did speak, it seemed a rebuke, for Job didn't pass every test. Yet, Job made it!

There will come a day when physical pain, emotional hurt, an attack of our faith, some terrible disappointment, or some horrendous news will come our way. Since our response is critical, what should we do? Here are some directives:

First, as an initial response, we should remain positive, as Job did, and we should refuse to succumb to self-pity. No matter how bad the circumstances, ours is probably not the worse-case scenario:

> Consider those who had it worse than our plight but survived. We have biblical examples: Joseph, Job, John the Baptist, Jesus. And we have more current examples all around us. One case in point is Nelson Mandela. He spent twenty-seven years of his life as a political prisoner, eighteen of those years in a tiny cell in the Robben Island prison, sleeping on a bedroll on concrete. During this time, he received

only one visit a year for thirty minutes, and he was allowed to receive and send only one letter every six months. Yet he survived without becoming bitter. Is our plight worse? Probably not, so we need to get up from our bed of self-pity and get going: we can start by worshiping the God Who oversees our plight!

Paul and Silas offer us a wonderful example of remaining positive during difficult times (Acts 16). In a Philippian jail, their feet in stocks and their backs raw from an illegal beating, there's an array of attitudes they could have adapted: anger, depression, fear, self-pity, and more. Instead of these, they chose to worship God. And God honored them. At midnight an earthquake rattled the prison walls, and the cell doors and the bands that bound the prisoners were unlatched. My wife says God became so excited about Paul and Silas' attitude that He did cartwheels in heaven, which produced the quake.

Attitude is always a choice. And attitude always makes the difference in the outcome, not necessarily what happens to us but what our attitude does for us. A positive attitude keeps the heart and mind on track. It's difficult to love God with all our heart, mind, and strength when we are angry, or depressed, or fearful, or full of self-pity. These emotions take too much energy. Conversely, when we approach difficulties with a grateful heart, this attitude facilitates our relationship with God. "For with God nothing shall be impossible" (Luke 1:37).

Second, we need to respond to difficult circumstances using our

There Will Come A Day

God-given resources. We have far more resources than Job had, and he made it, so, we can also. Consider the four resources we have:

We have God's Word: We have Jesus as our example regarding the use of God's Word to combat the adversary. He went to the Word during his temptation: "It is written," He told the tempter. We need to quote the words of our Lord: "Get thee behind me, Satan: for it is written, Thou shalt worship the Lord thy God, and him only shalt thou serve" (Luke 4:8). Build your defense and offense on Bible promises, for God is faithful to His Word. He honors His promises. So, proclaim and claim the Word. Memorize and quote specific Scriptures:

> I can do all things through Christ which strengtheneth me.
>
> Philippians 4:13

> There hath no temptation taken you but such as is common to man: but God is faithful, who will not suffer you to be tempted above that ye are able; but will with the temptation also make a way to escape, that ye may be able to bear it.
>
> 1 Corinthians 10:13

> He that dwelleth in the secret place of the most High shall abide under the shadow of the Almighty.
>
> Psalm 91:1

> I will say of the Lord, He is my refuge and my

fortress: my God; in him will I trust. Surely he shall deliver thee ...

Psalm 91.2-3

A thousand shall fall at thy side, and ten thousand at thy right hand; but it shall not come nigh thee. Because thou hast made the Lord, which is my refuge, even the most High, thy habitation; There shall no evil befall thee, neither shall any plague come nigh thy dwelling. For he shall give his angels charge over thee, to keep thee in all thy ways.

Psalm 91:7-11

No weapon that is formed against thee shall prosper ...

Isaiah 54:17

We have the Holy Spirit baptism: The same force that created the universe dwells in us. We have the example of the apostles, who—though beaten and threatened—prayed, and the place was shaken by the power of God. And the power of the Holy Ghost gave them boldness to preach in the face of adversity (Acts 4:31). We have the ability to pray in the Spirit. When we pray in the Spirit language, it is God speaking through us, so it is difficult for Satan to mount an offense against the power of God; rather, he is reduced to a defensive mode. We have a voice both in heaven and earth pleading for us: the Sacrificial Lamb in heaven at the throne of God and the Spirit of Christ residing within us on earth.

Who is he that condemneth? It is Christ that died, yea

There Will Come A Day

rather, that is risen again, who is even at the right hand of God, who also maketh intercession for us.

Romans 8:34

My little children, these things write I unto you, that ye sin not. And if any man sin, we have an advocate with the Father, Jesus Christ the righteous: And he is the propitiation for our sins: and not for ours only, but also for the sins of the whole world.

1 John 2:1-2

Likewise the Spirit also helpeth our infirmities: for we know not what we should pray for as we ought: but the Spirit itself maketh intercession for us with groanings which cannot be uttered.

Romans 8:26

We have the name of Jesus: "Plead the name!" the old-timers said. What did they mean by that? Call on the all-powerful name of Jesus to take over the situation.

Wherefore God also hath highly exalted him, and given him a name which is above every name: That at the name of Jesus every knee should bow, of things in heaven, and things in earth, and things under the earth…

Philippians 2:9-10

We have the church: This resource offers an array of blessings. The church, which is the "body of Christ" (1 Corinthians 12:27), binds with us in praying for our needs. The ministers within the church are authorized by Christ to fight for us. To the apostle with the keys to the Kingdom of God, Jesus said: "Verily I say unto you, Whatsoever ye shall bind on earth shall be bound in heaven: and whatsoever ye shall loose on earth shall be loosed in heaven" (Matthew 18:18).

A sermon on Sunday is but one part of the responsibility and authority of ministry. They have been commissioned to equip us to stand against "the wiles of the devil" (Ephesians 6:11), and they are authorized to "stand in the gap" against the judgment of God if we fail (Ezekiel 22:30). Consider the authority of the church:

> But if I tarry long, that thou mayest know how thou oughtest to behave thyself in the house of God, which is the church of the living God, the pillar and ground of the truth.
>
> 1 Timothy 3:15

Christ empowers the church with the Gifts of the Spirit (1 Corinthians 12 and 14). The church has an altar (Hebrews 13:10) on which the perfect sacrifice—Christ—has paid our debt of sin (Hebrews 13:12). Consider the significance of the altar: When Hezekiah received a threatening letter from the invading Assyrians, he went to the house of God, spread out the letter before God (which is what we do at the altar when we open our hearts to Christ), and he talked to God. God dispatched one angel and demolished the army of Assyria (2 Kings 19).

There Will Come A Day

Without doubt, a day will come when adversity seems to reign. It is imperative we recognize God is always in the midst of the storms that come against us. This account in the Old Testament offers direction (2 Kings 6). Elisha's servant brought him a report, "We're surrounded by the enemy," but Elijah responded, "Don't be afraid, there are more with us than with them." Elisha prayed, "Open his eyes, Lord, that he may see." What was the servant not seeing? Yes, the enemy surrounded them, but all around their enemy were horses and chariots of fire because, "The angel of the Lord encampeth round about them that fear him, and delivereth them" (Psalm 34:7).

But why does a loving God allow such trials among His people? Paul answered this in a letter to the church at Philippi. "That ye may be blameless and harmless, the sons of God, without rebuke, in the midst of a crooked and perverse nation, among whom ye shine as lights in the world" (Philippians 2:15). My wife scribbled a note in our devotional alongside this verse: "Stars are made from explosions—they are broken—so that they shine. Don't fear brokenness." True, stars are an accumulation of dust and gas which collapses due to gravity. In the process, they ignite and shine like our sun. And the residue of the birth of this new sun forms planets that revolve around it.[1] Our brokenness and coming forth from the fiery trial paves the way for others to triumph. "Then shall the righteous shine forth as the sun in the kingdom of their Father..." (Matthew 13:43). And like the wise men at Christ's birth, our fellowmen sometimes need a bright star to lead them to the Savior.

Unfortunately, when things don't go well, too often we

momentarily forget God's address. This was the case with Job: "Oh that I knew where I might find Him..." (Job 23:3), Job lamented. That's us when bad things happen: Where are you Lord? Have you moved and didn't leave a forwarding address? No, God has not moved; conversely, He's still receiving mail at 101 Altar Avenue. And prayer is still working! How do I know? It worked in Bible days! The enemy surrounded Jerusalem and sent a threatening letter to Hezekiah, a letter that challenged God's power to deliver His people. Hezekiah forwarded the letter to God. And God went into action. God has not changed (Hebrews 13:8). Is the enemy sending you threatening notices? Is your adversary challenging your faith? Is sickness ravaging your body. Just like Hezekiah of old, it's time to send a note to Jesus Christ at 101 Altar Avenue. "Dear Lord ... ." You finish your letter.

Further, God's address at 101 Bible Boulevard is still active. Again, how do I know? The Bible says so (Isaiah 40:8; Jeremiah 5:14; Matthew 4:4; 24:35; Hebrews 4:12). The devil thought he had Jesus in a defeated state, so he proceeded to make demands, but Jesus stopped him in his tracks by saying: "It is written ... ." Jesus doesn't like His Word distorted and He certainly expects it to be used correctly. I'm thinking of another account in Scripture (John 8). The accusers flung her at Jesus' feet. "The Law demands death to this adulteress," they demanded. They had intended to deliver her to 101 Judgment Junction but somewhere made a wrong turn and ended up at 101 Bible Boulevard. When Jesus heard their accusations, He stooped and wrote in the sands of mercy. Fortunately for us all, no sin written in the sands of mercy can survive over time, for the grace of Calvary erases our confessed sins every time.

There Will Come A Day

Have you time for one more example? Their backs ached from the merciless beating, and flies mingled with blood oozing through their garments. Intense pain prevented sleep, so still up at midnight, Paul and Silas decided to send a message to an address they had used many times before: 101 Praise Plaza (Acts 16). Need I go on? God has not moved away. He's at the same address, and you can get in touch with Him today and everyday. He always answers His mail.

There will "come a day," but no matter when that day comes, you will survive because you approach every day with worship, prayer, praise, and the quoting and believing of Scriptures. And when tragedy strikes, some of the first calls you make will be to Christian friends who will support you with prayer and words of encouragement. And one of the first places you will go to is the church, where you will receive spiritual guidance. And one of your safest places in all the world is the altar, where Jesus will meet you with loving arms of comfort and strength.

Note: In this sermon, the author used a visual by having a group of teens pretend to bully a small child. They surrounded him, pushing and taunting. Then he had some of the tallest men in the church surround the bullying circle, and the praise team sang: "It may look like I'm surrounded, but I'm surrounded by you …. this is how I fight my battles."[2]

You Matter To God: A Book Of Sermons

Endnotes
1) How Do Stars Form, Majken Brahe Ellegaard Christensen, Frontiers for Young Minds, Published July 4, 2019
2) Michael W. Smith, Surrounded, 2018

This I Know

We find phrases in Scripture similar to this title that are significant. These phrases include: This I Know; I am persuaded; For I know; We know. Contrary to those who propose there are no absolutes, we understand there are certain statements we can be sure are absolutes because they are in the Scripture. I would like us to consider five such truths: 1) God is the designer, creator, and sustainer of mankind; 2) God became man in order to redeem us; 3) since the God of Scripture is our Lord, we are obligated to Him; 4) this world will end; 5) there will be a final judgment.

While traveling on the interstate, four letters spray-painted on a concrete column caught my attention: USMC. I readily assumed they stood for the United States Marine Corps. If this assumption was correct, there are still a number of things about this particular graffiti that I don't know:

- I don't know who spray-painted them, nor do I know anything about their background: whether they are male or female, their age, ethnicity, their IQ (though I assume it to be low).
- I don't know the motive: What prompted someone to bring a can of spray-paint and walk along the expressway until he/she found a column and then risked being arrested to spray-paint in great big letters, USMC?

- I don't know if this act was in anger, in jest, or in admiration.

There is, however, one thing I know about the defacing of that public property: those letters were not spray-painted by a genuine Marine. How do I know this? Because of their code of honor.

Three Core Values of Marine Corps
- Honor: This is the bedrock of our character. It is the quality that empowers Marines to exemplify the ultimate in ethical and moral behavior: never to lie, cheat, or steal; to abide by an uncompromising code of integrity; to respect human dignity; and to have respect and concern for each other. It represents the maturity, dedication, trust, and dependability that commit Marines to act responsibly, be accountable for their actions, fulfill their obligations, and hold others accountable for their actions.
- Courage: This is the heart of their Core Values. Courage is the mental, moral, and physical strength ingrained in Marines that sees them through the challenges of combat and the mastery of fear. These values motivate them to do what is right, to adhere to a high standard of personal conduct, to lead by example, and to make tough decisions under stress and pressure. It is the inner strength that enables a Marine to take that extra step.
- Commitment: This is the spirit of determination and dedication within members of a force of arms

This I Know

that leads to professionalism and mastery of the art of war. It promotes the highest order of discipline for unit and self and is the ingredient that instills dedication to Corps and country twenty-four hours a day, creating concern for others, and creating an unrelenting determination to achieve a standard of excellence in every endeavor. Commitment is the value that establishes the Marine as the warrior and citizen others strive to emulate.

No, I don't think this graffiti was spray-painted by a legitimate Marine: maybe a disillusioned Marine, or perhaps a dishonorably discharged Marine trying to prove something, or a wannabe Marine confused about the definition of courage and honor and commitment. But this was definitely not a true Marine. This we know about whoever it was that defaced public property to spray-paint USMC.

The same analogy can be said about Christianity: some things we can know beyond a shadow of a doubt. How can we be so sure? It's in God's Word, and God's Word is true, for Jesus said, "Heaven and earth shall pass away: but my words shall never pass away" (Mark 13:31).

Let's suppose you want to be a nuclear physicist. You don't simply come up with your own philosophy of physics (which includes more than one field), but you first study all the discoveries that have ever been made and recorded regarding physics. Using this thought regarding Christianity, the true Christian faith is predicated upon the Bible: not tradition, not history, not opinion, not what I want it to be. Why? For the Bible is our manual regarding God. It is the bedrock of the Christian faith. What we know about God is written in the Bible. It's the safest book regarding God's existence, His character, His story, and His plans for the future.

Fox News carried an article by Pastor Andy Stanley entitled, *Five reasons people leave the church*. The article's number one reason? We tell people that the Bible is the basis of Christianity. The article explains that many believe the Bible is the foundation of our religion, but Pastor Stanley explains, the Bible is not the foundation for our religion, Jesus is. I believe this statement needs qualified, but before I go off on the pastor's comment, there is an awesome truth he is promoting, for Jesus did saw: "I am the way and the truth and the life ..." (John 14:6).

I think I understand what Pastor Stanley meant in this article, but without another truth alongside this statement, this concept allows for all kinds of assumptions, lifestyles, and false doctrines. How so? Because Christianity is then based upon what anyone thinks they know about Jesus. So long as we are sincere, we can create our own Jesus while sipping from a bottle of beer in between puffing on a marijuana joint. Such loose terms for a relationship with Christ attacks Scripture and its relevancy. I'm reminded of what the Scripture says: "Beloved, when I gave all diligence to write unto you of the common salvation, it was needful for me to write unto you, and exhort you that ye should earnestly contend for the faith which was once delivered unto the saints" (Jude 1:3). We must contend for the Bible's significance. But isn't Jesus the most important person in the Bible? Of course! But what we know about Jesus we learn

This I Know

from the Bible; therefore, what we experience in Christ needs to align with biblical truth. How we live for Christ needs more than personal supposition about Christianity; our Christian lifestyle needs scriptural sanction.

When we veer from Scripture, even as a professing Christian, there's no telling where we will end up. We have preachers emphasizing their points by cursing from the pulpit and proclaiming that we don't need to read an ancient book called the Bible to get relevant answers for todays' problems. We have gospel singers who commit adultery, have multiple children out of wedlock, divorce, re-marry, and continue singing and selling their gospel albums, sometimes with little or no consequences among the Christian community. We have rising stars whose recordings go to the top on the charts, but it doesn't matter about their provocative, low-cut, off-the-shoulders attire. Such biblical issues seem to no longer matter because the person is singing about Jesus, and they are sincere. So, modesty, moderateness, and even morality are tossed aside because they're terms from an ancient book that is considered by too many Christians as being out-of-touch and irrelevant for today's seeker-friendly church. And these high-profile individuals become our Christian youth's idols and role models. Sad to say, lyrics and a sincere presentation often take precedent over what the Bible says: after all, it's a really old book, written by really old men who lived a long time ago in a different culture. Really? Are you kidding me? Have we drifted this far? Many church cultures have, and they justify much by one's sincerity. However, sincerity is not the litmus test for Christianity: God's Word is the only safe basis for our beliefs. I am inclined to believe at some point in his life that Jim

Jones was sincere. But what he coerced followers to do is insanely contrary to Scripture.

Yes, Pastor Stanley is correct, Jesus is the foundation upon which the church is built. But the Bible is the only existing book that tells us what we need to know about Jesus. Our experience with Christ must be based upon Scripture. To veer from Scripture regarding this issue can cause two problems. First, we may receive less of Christ than He offers, such as the Holy Spirit baptism which is promised by Christ: "And I will pray the Father, and he shall give you another Comforter, that he may abide with you for ever" (John 14:16). Many settle for making a verbal acceptance of Christ, with no reciprocation on the part of Christ. Yet the encounter of the Holy Spirit baptism in the New Birth experience is a vital part of Scripture. Jesus admonished Nicodemus: "... Verily, verily, I say unto thee, Except a man be born of water and of the Spirit, he cannot enter into the kingdom of God" (John 3:5). The Bible gives us a play-by-play visual of the Holy Spirit baptism:

> And when the day of Pentecost was fully come, they were all with one accord in one place. And suddenly there came a sound from heaven as of a rushing mighty wind, and it filled all the house where they were sitting. And there appeared unto them cloven tongues like as of fire, and it sat upon each of them. And they were all filled with the Holy Ghost, and began to speak with other tongues, as the Spirit gave them utterance.
>
> Acts 2:1-4

This I Know

Now when the apostles which were at Jerusalem heard that Samaria had received the word of God, they sent unto them Peter and John: Who, when they were come down, prayed for them, that they might receive the Holy Ghost: (For as yet he was fallen upon none of them: only they were baptized in the name of the Lord Jesus.) Then laid they their hands on them, and they received the Holy Ghost.

Acts 8:14-17

While Peter yet spake these words, the Holy Ghost fell on all them which heard the word. And they of the circumcision which believed were astonished, as many as came with Peter, because that on the Gentiles also was poured out the gift of the Holy Ghost. For they heard them speak with tongues, and magnify God. Then answered Peter, Can any man forbid water, that these should not be baptized, which have received the Holy Ghost as well as we?

Acts 10:44-47

And it came to pass, that, while Apollos was at Corinth, Paul having passed through the upper coasts came to Ephesus: and finding certain disciples, He said unto them, Have ye received the Holy Ghost since ye believed? And they said unto him, We have not so much as heard whether there be any Holy Ghost. And he said unto them, Unto what then were ye baptized? And they said, Unto John's baptism. Then said Paul,

> John verily baptized with the baptism of repentance, saying unto the people, that they should believe on him which should come after him, that is, on Christ Jesus. When they heard this, they were baptized in the name of the Lord Jesus. And when Paul had laid his hands upon them, the Holy Ghost came on them; and they spake with tongues, and prophesied.
>
> Acts 19:1-6

There is a second problem that can happen if we do not anchor our beliefs in scriptural accuracy. We may fall into false doctrine, succumb to worldliness, become bitter at heart, or even lapse into goofiness. I've seen online posts of colleagues I believe are sincere, but they have veered from some basic tenants of Scripture, and in so doing, they have lapsed into utter goofiness and confusion. They tend to think themselves to always have a word from the Lord, to the point that they can't sit in an airport and have a Coke without propping their iPhones on the table to video themselves giving an exposition of some great revelation they received while napping on the plane: often utter goofiness. Because they have veered from scriptural directives, some have allowed bitterness to take root, failing to submit to spiritual authority and accountability (as if those who care for them are trying to hold them back from doing great things for Jesus). And others become puffed up, allowing a prideful heart to dominate their actions.

How do we stay on course? We must allow the Bible to be the primary source of our knowledge about God. The Apostle Peter described the Bible as " ... the word of God, which liveth and abideth

This I Know

forever ... the word of the Lord endureth forever" (1 Peter 1:23, 25). Instead of causing you to drift down a path of self-destruction, the eternal truths of Scripture will draw you nearer to Christ's wounded side and will soften your spirit so that others may come alongside you to offer direction or even challenge your direction. Let's consider five points from the Scripture that are extremely important in staying on course.

1) God is the designer, creator, and sustainer of mankind.

How do we know this? It's a Bible truth. "In the beginning God created the heaven and the earth" (Genesis 1:1). If we waffle here, then many other truths will crumble, unable to withstand the storms of philosophy, doubt, temptation, and disappointment. Every other significant truth can be shaken if we do not believe that God was our Creator. Either God created us, and we are ultimately responsible to Him, or it happened some other way. If it happened some other way, perhaps we can do what we want, make up our rules to please our fancy, and go our way without any temporal or eternal consequences. But the Bible says differently: "For by him were all things created, that are in heaven, and that are in earth, visible and invisible, whether they be thrones, or dominions, or principalities, or powers: all things were created by him, and for him" (Colossians 1:16). We have to get this: "by Him" and "for Him."

2) God became man in order to redeem us.

Mankind sinned, lost his place in the garden, and lost his favor with God, but it did not diminish God's love for His creation. In order to redeem mankind from sin, God became a man, and though sinless, submitted to a cruel death at Calvary to pay for mankind's sins. How do we know this? The Scriptures say such.

> In the beginning was the Word, and the Word was with God, and the Word was God.... He came unto his own, and his own received him not. But as many as received him, to them gave he power to become the sons of God, even to them that believe on his name: Which were born, not of blood, nor of the will of the flesh, nor of the will of man, but of God. And the Word was made flesh, and dwelt among us, (and we beheld his glory, the glory as of the only begotten of the Father,) full of grace and truth.
>
> John 1:1, 11-14

> Take heed therefore unto yourselves, and to all the flock, over the which the Holy Ghost hath made you overseers, to feed the church of God, which he hath purchased with his own blood.
>
> Acts 20:28

Here's the mystery of the ages. God, Who is a Spirit, Who no one could look upon and live, saved us with His own blood: not the blood of an animal sacrifice, but His own blood. How? God became a man.

> For unto us a child is born, unto us a son is given: and the government shall be upon his shoulder ...
>
> Isaiah 9:6

This I Know

But in this mystery, He was, and He remained, the God of the universe.

> ... and his name shall be called Wonderful, Counsellor, The mighty God, The everlasting Father, The Prince of Peace.
>
> Isaiah 9:6

> And without controversy great is the mystery of godliness: God was manifest in the flesh, justified in the Spirit, seen of angels, preached unto the Gentiles, believed on in the world, received up into glory.
>
> 1 Timothy 3:16

3) Since the God of Scripture is our Lord, we are obligated to Him.

As a Christian, God demands two things of us: faith and obedience. Multiple examples in Scripture reveal these two obligations: trust and obey—just like the old hymn says. When Israel marched against Jericho, these two rules dominated the instructions of God to Joshua. Two things I need from you, Joshua: faith and obedience.
- Faith: Believe that God will tear down the walls, so shut up and get in step. Today is no different: we are to trust God. Sadly, many times we not only distrust, but we also challenge God and proudly post our rebellious thoughts for all to read.
- Obedience: Don't take any of the accursed things, leave them for Me, the Lord instructed Joshua. If you

take the accursed things into your tent they will pollute you, but I can handle them: once in my presence they become sanctified. It's as if God recognized we can't handle the things of the world. And here's where we waffle: we assume God doesn't want me to have fun, to prosper, to be successful. Those thoughts aren't true, but this statement is: God's number one priority for us is trying to get us to heaven. If we believe Him and obey Him, we will make it to heaven!

4) This world will end.

Almost two thousand years ago, the Apostle Peter prophetically wrote that this world shall end. Scientists agree, but they say it will end millions of years down the road. Do we believe the urgency of Scripture, or do we acquiesce to the teaching of science, even though science is sometimes in opposition to Scripture? To accept science over Scripture is to embark into humanism: attaching significance to human reasoning over that of our Divine Creator.

Since only God knows the time frame for the earth's future, let's believe His Word and accept the urgency of Scripture. Here's the Bible time line: The rapture (or catching away of the church, which could happen any day); seven years of devastation upon the Earth (called the Great Tribulation); Christ's return to the Earth to bind Satan and cast him into the bottomless pit and to set up a thousand-year peaceful reign on the Earth; Satan is released for a short time and then cast into the lake of fire for eternity; the Earth as we know it is destroyed, and a new Earth is created; the New Jerusalem (the

This I Know

celestial city of God prepared for His people) descends upon the New Earth and eternity begins.

The Apostle Peter emphasized the urgency of the end-time.

> But the day of the Lord will come as a thief in the night; in the which the heavens shall pass away with a great noise, and the elements shall melt with fervent heat, the earth also and the works that are therein shall be burned up... .Looking for and hasting unto the coming of the day of God, wherein the heavens being on fire shall be dissolved, and the elements shall melt with fervent heat? Nevertheless we, according to his promise, look for new heavens and a new earth, wherein dwelleth righteousness.
>
> 2 Peter 3:10, 12-13

The above Scriptures don't sound like the earth has a million years of existence left; conversely, they ring loud with urgency.

5) There will be a final judgment.

In spite of the fact that God is love and full of mercy, and He is not willing that any should perish but wants everyone to be saved (2 Peter 3:9), there will be a final judgment of all mankind, and eternal damnation is the final destiny for many.

> And I saw a great white throne, and him that sat on it, from whose face the earth and the heaven fled away;

and there was found no place for them. And I saw the dead, small and great, stand before God; and the books were opened: and another book was opened, which is the book of life: and the dead were judged out of those things which were written in the books, according to their works. And the sea gave up the dead which were in it; and death and hell delivered up the dead which were in them: and they were judged every man according to their works. And death and hell were cast into the lake of fire. This is the second death. And whosoever was not found written in the book of life was cast into the lake of fire.

Revelation 20:11-15

Unless we believe the Scripture, we veer into all kinds of explanations as to life after death: rationalizing, denying, and justifying. I spoke with a friend the other day who has drifted from an experience in Christ into this foggy realm of vindication for his life apart from Christ. He explained how he intends to meet his Maker: cremation and his remains placed inside a cross-decorated urn. His reasoning? If the cremation doesn't prevent final judgment, then the cross etched on the urn may buy him passage into heaven. He's placed his eternal future on a scheme he's concocted apart from God's holy Scripture. When we consider God's Word as our guidebook, the concepts of Christianity often take on a completely different sense than those of tradition and human reasoning. And the Bible is the foundation upon which we can safely and confidently build our lives. Didn't Jesus say something like that? "Therefore whosoever heareth these sayings of mine, and doeth them, I will

This I Know

liken him unto a wise man, which built his house upon a rock" (Matthew 7:24). Interestingly, this statement follows a sobering sermon of Christ:

> Enter ye in at the strait gate: for wide is the gate, and broad is the way, that leadeth to destruction, and many there be which go in thereat: Because strait is the gate, and narrow is the way, which leadeth unto life, and few there be that find it. Beware of false prophets, which come to you in sheep's clothing, but inwardly they are ravening wolves. Ye shall know them by their fruits. Do men gather grapes of thorns, or figs of thistles? Even so every good tree bringeth forth good fruit; but a corrupt tree bringeth forth evil fruit. A good tree cannot bring forth evil fruit, neither can a corrupt tree bring forth good fruit. Every tree that bringeth not forth good fruit is hewn down, and cast into the fire. Wherefore by their fruits ye shall know them. Not every one that saith unto me, Lord, Lord, shall enter into the kingdom of heaven; but he that doeth the will of my Father which is in heaven. Many will say to me in that day, Lord, Lord, have we not prophesied in thy name? and in thy name have cast out devils? and in thy name done many wonderful works? And then will I profess unto them, I never knew you: depart from me, ye that work iniquity.
>
> Matthew 7:13-23

I fear for my friend who thinks he's figured out a way around the endgame. And we all should have a godly concern of eternal damnation. And though we would like to dismiss such, it's a reality of Scripture.

These five truths I know: God is the designer, creator, and sustainer of mankind; God became man in order to redeem us; since the God of Scripture is our Lord, we are obligated to Him; this world will end; there will be a final judgment. These five truths, believed and obeyed, bring a different perspective to how we view life: a few years versus eternity. But how can I be sure of these five concepts regarding God? The Bible tells me so.

Time To Come Home

Jesus Christ has the right to first place in our hearts: by His right as our Creator and the earned right as our Redeemer. We belong to Him because our very breath comes from His creative genius and sustaining love; further, even though mankind sold his soul to Satan, Christ bought us back at the awful expense of Calvary. It's not unrealistic when Jesus instructed:

> Jesus said unto him, Thou shalt love the Lord thy God with all thy heart, and with all thy soul, and with all thy mind.
>
> Matthew 22:37

> No man can serve two masters: for either he will hate the one, and love the other; or else he will hold to the one, and despise the other. Ye cannot serve God and mammon.
>
> Matthew 6:24

> Love not the world, neither the things that are in the world. If any man love the world, the love of the Father is not in him. For all that is in the world, the lust of the flesh, and the lust of the eyes, and the pride of life, is not of the Father, but is of the world. And

> the world passeth away, and the lust thereof: but he that doeth the will of God abideth for ever.
>
> 1 John 2:15-17

I shudder when I read what the Bible says regarding the consequences of our lack of commitment to Christ.

> And I saw a great white throne, and him that sat on it, from whose face the earth and the heaven fled away; and there was found no place for them. And I saw the dead, small and great, stand before God; and the books were opened: and another book was opened, which is the book of life: and the dead were judged out of those things which were written in the books, according to their works. And the sea gave up the dead which were in it; and death and hell delivered up the dead which were in them: and they were judged every man according to their works. And death and hell were cast into the lake of fire. This is the second death. And whosoever was not found written in the book of life was cast into the lake of fire.
>
> Revelation 20:11-15

Life is much more serious than we care to accept. The reality of the consequences of sin is greater than we want to believe, but that does not change the Word of God. The old adage, "As you make your bed, you've got to sleep in it," is not a verse in the Bible, but it is the theme of Scripture from Genesis to Revelation: from Adam and Eve to the last person born. There is a consequence for every

Time To Come Home

wrong action; however, there is a Savior who offered Himself on a cross to suffer the consequences of our sins and leave us guiltless. Many never accept such, and far too many have walked away from Christ's love and grace. Eternal judgment awaits them. There is no other option for salvation than Christ's grace offered to us.

I recall a moving article where the writer shared an interview which he had many years ago with famed American author Ernest Hemingway.[1] Some of Mr. Hemingway's more famous books are: *A Farewell to Arms, For Whom the Bell Tolls,* and *The Old Man and the Sea,* but none of these seem more intriguing than Hemingway's revelation of his personal heartbreak. In this interview, Hemingway bared his soul and shared his loss and his regrets for a decision he made early on in life. He explained that he was in love with two women at the same time: his wife and a wealthy party girl that seemed to land wherever he happened to be writing.

> His wife Hadley was devoted to him during their early years of poverty, before he became famous. She was the mother to his first and favorite son. Her marriage to him could be summed up in a single word: faithful. Not so with him. While married to Hadley, Hemingway hung out with a wealthy party girl who felt she could buy anything she wanted, or that he wanted. Perhaps intrigued by Mr. Hemingway, she made herself available to him when he went on location to write: Paris, Cuba, Switzerland. She literally bought Hemingway's attention.

Hadley eventually got tired of Hemingway's adultery and left him. It wasn't easy in those days for him to acquire a divorce without her consent, and since she wasn't ready to consent to a divorce, they remained married but separated. One day, when he stopped by her house to pick up their son, she asked if they could talk. She shared a written contract as terms for them to divorce. The agreement stated: "If for one hundred days you cease to see your girlfriend, and if after the hundred days you still say you love her, then I will give you a divorce." They both signed the agreement.

During this time, a friend tried to reason with Hemingway and help patch up his marriage but to no avail. Each day Hemingway marked an 'X' on the calendar date, eagerly awaiting his divorce and being able to reunite with his girlfriend.

On the seventy-first day of the agreement, to his surprise, he received a letter from his wife. She explained, "Since it's obvious a divorce is what you want, I will grant it." Though he wanted the divorce, he expressed in the interview that the contents of the letter broke his heart.

Per his interview, life did not go well for him after he and Hadley divorced. He ended up going through three divorces. He lived a life of misery and regret. In retrospect, he had lost the one person he truly loved,

Time To Come Home

Hadley, because he would not commit only to her.

Mr. Hemingway spent a lifetime trying to get back what he gave away: true love. He recalled in this interview how he would see someone he thought was his first wife, and he would follow her, only to be disappointed when he realized it was not Hadley. In fact, he saw Hadley only once after their divorce. As he sat on a terrace in Paris, a taxi pulled up and Hadley got out. He rushed to her and they embraced. She joined him at his table, and they talked for a few minutes, catching up.

"I follow you in the newspapers," she said with a smile. "Farewell to Arms" was a wonderful story.

He responded, "I think about you often. You're my inspiration for every woman I write about. You believed in me. I'll spend the rest of my life looking for you."

"And I'll always love you," she said. Then, glancing at her watch, she stood and explained, "I must be going to my appointment."

"Can we meet sometime for dinner?" he asked.

She did not respond.

"No sinister motive," he said. "I just want to look at you across the table for a little while."

She declined the invitation.

Mr. Hemingway concluded the interview with a sad note. "I walked her to the street corner. I watched as she disappeared into the crowd. That was the last time I saw her."

His fourth wife says it was an accident, but many conclude Ernest Hemingway committed suicide, devastated by the loss of a life that could have been. But worse still are the eternal souls separated from the God Who gave His life to redeem them.

Hey, wayward husband, prodigal son, strong-willed daughter, don't you think it's about time you come home? While there is still time, don't you think you should step back across the threshold into the loving arms of your Savior?

Hey, soul straying from the fold, what if the Lord gave you a contract of one hundred days to see if you love Him or the world? Would you run out the allotted time before deciding? What would your calendar look like?
- Day 1: I've got 99 days left; plenty of time.
- Day 5: No need to get in a hurry. Christ will be there when I'm ready to return.
- Day 10: I'll enjoy my allotted time in the world.
- Day 70: Thirty days left before I have to decide.

Time To Come Home

Wayward pilgrim, you're close to finding out that the world can't satisfy you in the end, and unless you give your heart completely to Christ, you cannot have the relationship He desires with you.

I'm not suggesting the Lord is quick to leave us, but I do believe there is a day coming when He cannot tolerate our rejection of His love. The throne of judgment will be the last time many will see Him, and they will spend eternity regretting their decision.

If you don't believe in a literal hell (a lake of fire as described in Scripture), even though I do, then at least consider that there is a place prepared for all those who don't make it to heaven. Call this place whatever you want, but consider, the alternative to heaven (whatever you call it) at its best will be a place filled with the most undesirable of people: mass murderers, rapists, thieves, liars. Who is the worst person you can think of? He or she will be there. You don't want to be in that place. Neither does the Lord want you to go there.

Time is running out. It's time to come home. It's time to commit to Christ as Lord of your life. His is a love no one can duplicate and no one can equal. To walk away from His love is to live a lifetime of regret, knowing what could have been.

Endnote
1) Interview of Ernest Hemingway by A. E. Hotchner, Smithsonian Magazine, October 2015

When We Talk To Ourselves

And he spake a parable unto them, saying, The ground of a certain rich man brought forth plentifully: And he thought within himself, saying, What shall I do, because I have no room where to bestow my fruits? And he said, This will I do: I will pull down my barns, and build greater; and there will I bestow all my fruits and my goods. And I will say to my soul, Soul, thou hast much goods laid up for many years; take thine ease, eat, drink, and be merry. But God said unto him, Thou fool, this night thy soul shall be required of thee: then whose shall those things be, which thou hast provided?"

Luke 12:16-20

I can't recall the source of a story I read years ago, but it gripped my heart and has never let go. Here's my recollection:

> On his way home, Thomas Benson purchased a bouquet of flowers. There is a gleam in his eyes. He has come home for a celebration. Today is his anniversary. No, not a wedding anniversary, nor a birthday, but it is a special day that he had started some twenty years prior. Though Mrs. Benson had

forgotten, he had not, for he had lived every day the past twenty years to see this day. It was twenty years ago that he and his wife Susan had opened their savings account—not just any account—it was a retirement account. And ever since, each Friday he had entrusted his paycheck to his best friend, his loving wife, and she would pay their bills, then deposit a certain amount in their retirement fund. By his calculations, he would now be able to take his retirement, and they would enjoy together all the things that previously they had only dreamed about.

He had worked hard for an unappreciative boss. Many were the days he was tempted to quit. Often, he would come home from a tiring and frustrating day, angry beyond endurance, but he would work off his angst by writing out his letter of resignation. Then he would file it away and let it be merely practice for the letter he would someday write. And that day had finally come!

Thomas handed the bouquet to his wife. "If my calculations are right," he said, "and I'm sure they are, I'll write the real letter of resignation tonight. Never again will I have to hear the cursing, the accusations, and the unappreciative comments of a bullying boss. Tonight, we celebrate our retirement."

At first she accepted the bouquet and offered a

When We Talk To Ourselves

congratulatory smile. Then she flung herself at his feet, and through anguished sobs, she broke forth the terrible news that there was not enough money in the savings for him to retire. She had spent some! "How much?" he asked. "Most of it," she replied. While he had toiled through long hours these many years, up at 4:30, arriving home often after sunset, she had been dipping into the retirement savings.

Mr. Benson pulled away from her grasp. Can you see the anguish upon his face as he accepts the unimaginable? Do you hear his tired footsteps as he slowly retreats to his study? Do you see his trembling hands as he picks up a previously written letter of resignation, rips it into pieces, and tosses it into the fireplace. Do you feel his aching heart as he slumps into his chair, rests his chin in his hands, and stares blankly into the fire?

His best friend, his darling wife, had deceived him all these years. While he had planned and provided and sacrificed for their future, she had played and partied and spent most of their money.

What was she thinking all those years as she secretly lied to her husband? What did she tell herself each time she retrieved money from the savings? Surely she had to consider that this day would eventually come. In the silent stillness of the long wintry nights, surely she had to wrestle with her nagging conscience. What did she say when she talked to herself?

Mrs. Benson was not the first, nor will she be the last that talks rationale out the window.

- We don't know for sure what King David said to himself when he looked from his balcony into his neighbor's courtyard, but whatever it was, he was able to override a screaming conscience and plunge headlong into adultery, and ultimately to murder. (2 Samuel 11)
- We don't know for sure what Ananias and Sapphira told themselves as they plotted to deceive the Apostles. But we know what the Apostle said and what the Holy Spirit did. (Acts 5)
- Or what did Demas tell himself, as he sneaked away into the darkness of an alluring world? He had to do a lot of self-talk to drown out the soul-searching sermons of the Apostle Paul. What did he say when he talked himself back into the arms of the world? (2 Timothy 4:10)

We read what the rich man in Scripture said to himself: "... This will I do: I will pull down my barns, and build greater; and there will I bestow all my fruits and my goods. And I will say to my soul, Soul, thou hast much goods laid up for many years; take thine ease, eat, drink, and be merry" (Luke 12:18-19). And we also read what the Lord said to him: "... Thou fool, this night thy soul shall be required of thee: then whose shall those things be, which

When We Talk To Ourselves

thou hast provided?" (Luke 12:20). But what about us? We all talk to ourselves from time to time. It is a conversation of the heart. We may pretend, or even be convinced, that no one but self hears, but God hears. "And God saw that the wickedness of man was great in the earth, and that every imagination of the thoughts of his heart was only evil continually," (Genesis 6:5). And because God hears, He responds: "... it grieved him at his heart" (Genesis 6:6).

How does such deceptive self-talk happen? First, we conceive it. Then we contemplate it. Then we convince ourselves that it's okay. We blindly assume things will somehow work out okay in the end, but things do not just work out okay in the end. More often than not, the end is devastating. "Then when lust hath conceived, it bringeth forth sin: and sin, when it is finished, bringeth forth death" (James 1:15).

There needs to be much evaluation of our self-talk. Here are some questions to consider:
- What are some of the things we say when we talk to ourselves?
- What kind of soul do we expose by our self-talk?
- What deceptions are we having to battle to keep up our secret conversation?
- What lusts go unchecked in our hearts?
- What angers do we allow to roam throughout our minds?
- How does a Christian convince himself it's okay to take a drink of beer now and then when we consider what the Scripture says about wine, and what

statistics say about alcohol related deaths, and how we have seen it destroy families and friends?
- How does a Christian convince himself it's okay to watch an improper movie?
- How does a Christian convince himself it's proper to live in a co-ed dorm?
- How does a Christian nation convince its people that it's okay to have same sex bathrooms?
- How does a Christian young person convince himself that premarital sex is okay?
- How do Christians justify pornography?
- How have we as Americans convinced ourselves that the unborn have no rights, to the tune of over sixty-million abortions?
- How do Christians convince themselves it's okay to not invite guests to church? To withhold the tithe from the Lord? To never attend a weekly prayer meeting? To choose Wednesday night little league for their child over midweek Bible study?

We know what we say when we talk to ourselves. And if we're honest, we could even tell what the Lord is saying back to us from the Bible. But we override the truth and accept our deceptive heart as lord (Jeremiah 17:9).

Let's take this one step further. For some, your self-talk is keeping you beaten down. It is self-condemning. It is contrary to Scripture, which paints a wonderful picture of how God views His children. Motivational speaker Shad Helmstetter writes, "The

When We Talk To Ourselves

brain simply believes what you tell it most. And what you tell it about you, it will create. It has no choice."[1] Your self-talk needs to reflect God's Word, which says you are forgiven, you are loved, your sins have been removed as far as the east is from the west—which is indefinite. Therefore, speak faith. Faith talk will beget faith believing; faith believing will create faith in action. Faith in action creates results.

What do we say when we talk to ourselves about death? No matter what we say, the inevitable is all around us, and we can't talk our way out of death. Ten out of ten eventually die, and we all must stand before God and give an account. Our focus should be preparing to meet God. That conversation should include words of confession and faith in Calvary's redemption plan.

And right now, what are we saying to ourselves regarding salvation? Not today? Next Sunday? I'm not good enough? These are things we say week after week. But anything other than "Yes, Lord," is foolish. And let's remember what the Lord said: " … Thou fool, this night thy soul shall be required of thee …." (Luke 12:20). This night: not next week, or next year. This is a gamble we can't afford to lose.

Endnote
1) What To Say When You Talk To Yourself, Shad Helmstetter, Thorsons, 1991

You Can Do This

> Wherefore seeing we also are compassed about with so great a cloud of witnesses, let us lay aside every weight, and the sin which doth so easily beset us, and let us run with patience the race that is set before us, Looking unto Jesus ….
>
> Hebrews 12:1-2

It's an interesting society in which we live. Though heroes abound, and most people I rub shoulders with are ready to lend a helping hand, we have some who take advantage of our social structure. I find some people loudmouthed about their needs but wimpy about hard work that will supply their needs; some are self-centered, having everything but wanting more.

Most haven't had a disaster that toughens; contrariwise, there seems to be some kind of program to pad the pain of many problems. Here's a case in point: The US Environmental Protection Agency brought trauma counselors on board to help the workers deal with all the changes made by a new president. It's a society of "me first and no one else matters until my wants are supplied." A "What are you going to do for me?" mentality prevails in many places of employment. And when things get tough, that same mentality morphs into "I don't think I can do this. It's too difficult." There's one thing that societies before us have proven, that eighteen-year-olds marching off to war have shown, that explorers mapping out the unknown have experienced, and the endurance our forefathers have exhibited proves: "We can do this." No matter how tough the situation, with God we can make it.

In 2017, I attended the Presidential Inauguration with my son and grandson, . We stayed on the outskirts of the city, so we awoke at 4:30 to catch the closest subway, and we arrived in downtown DC about six in the morning. At the lengthy security check to enter the activities of the inauguration, we had to dispense all food and water. We stood for six hours in a cramped space: cold toes, muscles aching, and weak from hunger. After a while of endurance, my brain started screaming at me, "You Can't Do This." Before long I started to believe what my brain was telling me, and all I wanted to do was leave and find a comfortable place to sit down and warm my toes. But when the inauguration ceremony began, something happened within my body: energy renewed, feet warmed, and negativism left. Not only could I make it, but the event became exhilarating!

We all have to contend with that constant inner voice that sooner or later complains: "This is too difficult. The results aren't worth the sacrifice. I can't endure this." But I know differently. Yes, we can do this! So, let's consider how.

Every year, Australia hosts a 543.7 mile endurance race from Sydney to Melbourne. Professional runners consider this race among the world's most grueling ultra-marathons. Traditionally, the race takes five days to complete, and usually, only world-class athletes—who train specifically for the event—enter this race. These

You Can Do This

athletes are typically less than thirty years old and sponsored by large companies.

In 1983 a farmer named Cliff Young showed up at this race. Cliff was sixty-one years old and was not your typical observer: he wore overalls and work boots. To everyone's shock, Cliff wasn't there to observe. Surprisingly, he picked up his race number and joined the runners at the starting line.

The press and athletes told him, and observers thought it, "You're crazy, there's no way you can finish this race." To which he replied, "Yes, I can."

When the race started, the pros quickly left Cliff behind. The crowds and television audience were somewhat entertained by this newcomer to the race, as he didn't even run properly; conversely, he appeared to shuffle. Some feared for the old farmer's safety.

Knowing the race took five days to finish, the runners planned accordingly, hoping to be the first to sprint across the finish on the fifth day. They would run about eighteen hours a day and sleep for the remaining six hours. All except Cliff Young, for he hadn't planned things that way.

When the morning of the second day came, everyone

was in for a surprise. Not only was Cliff still in the race, he had continued jogging all through the night. While others slept, he kept running ... or should we say he kept shuffling. It was obvious he was not the fastest, but he never quit. And each day, while others caught a few hours of sleep, Cliff shuffled on through the night. At first it didn't seem to make much difference toward the outcome, but eventually, he came closer to the leading pack. And the final night, while the leaders dreamed of being first to cross the finish line, he surpassed all of those young, world-class athletes. The next day, to the amazement of all, he was the first finish. But wait, that's not all of the story. Not only did he finish first, he set a new course record.

How did he do it? He didn't listen to the criticism, the jests, the jokes, and the laughter when he started at a pace much slower than others; instead, he kept on running. He would not stop, and therefore, he finished. First.[1]

Too many Christians are listening to the wrong voices: the voice of defeatism, fear, discouragement, and deception of the adversary. And the loudest voice digs at our ego: someone is ahead of you, and you can't win. The results? We drop out of the race.

The baffled reporters asked Cliff Young, "How did you do it?" He explained:

You Can Do This

> "I grew up on a farm where we couldn't afford horses or tractors. So, the whole time I was growing up, whenever the storms rolled in, I'd have to go out and round up the sheep. We had two thousand sheep on two thousand acres. Sometimes I would have to run those sheep for two or three days. It took a long time, but I'd always catch them and bring them to safety."

Cliff knew he could run the race, even though he wasn't the fastest. And not only did he run, he won.

There are specific reasons Cliff won the 1983 Sydney endurance race. It was no accident; it was deliberate. He borrowed from life's experiences. His personal experiences gave him the confidence he needed to keep going. This is one of the reasons we need to engage in the study of Scripture: the Bible shares examples to encourage us that we, too, can make it. I'm thinking of young David's encounters with a lion and a bear: the practice runs. And then there was Goliath, the real race. Never despise life's lessons, no matter how trivial or inconvenient, they are preparing you for the race of a lifetime.

Cliff wouldn't quit. He picked up one foot and set it down a few inches in front of the other, and he continued the process mile after mile. No fancy moves. No short cuts. Boring? You bet. Tiring? Absolutely. But he kept doing what he knew he had to do to get across the finish line.

Cliff wasn't running for the $10,000 prize: he didn't even know about it. His was a deeper cause: completing the race. He kept his focus on the finish line. And in the end, he became the champion. And in the process, Cliff Young became a world changer. His style, called the Cliff Young shuffle, is mimicked by other runners today. Further, the race is now run without sleep, all because one man would not stop. Amazing!

Whatever race God has called you into, you can complete. God will not call you into a situation that's too difficult for you and Him working together. No matter what the adversary or your contemporaries or even what your own emotions may be saying, you can do this if God has called you.

You have an example set before you from both the Old and New Testaments that is beckoning: a great "cloud of witnesses" (Hebrews 12:1) . The dust-cloud from the shuffling feet of a thousand saintly runners says, "You can do this." You are trained by their example from the Holy Scripture. Can you hear Paul's proclamation as he walks the final steps to the executioner's block? "I can do all things through Christ which strengtheneth me" (Philippians 4:13). And like as with Paul, a hundred previous battles have toughened you for this race. You haven't begun to exhaust the potential of Scripture buried inside your head and heart. You're not going to listen to the wrong voices and get sidetracked. Further, you're going to lay aside the weights that hinder and the sins that beset: "that entangles" (Hebrews 12:1, NIV).

You must look to Jesus who encouraged us, "Come unto me, all ye that labour and are heavy laden, and I will give you rest" (Matthew 11:28). He has paved the way! He has the answers to all

You Can Do This

your doubts and questions. Ask! Seek! Knock! You are not running for material gain. There is something much more profound about this race. Pick up your foot and set it down in front of the other. One of those steps will eventually cross the finish line. And it will silence the naysayers, forever. Furthermore, it will inspire those following.

If we follow the directive of Scripture, we can do whatever God has called us to do. We can endure whatever circumstances life may throw our way. How do I know this? We're "... looking unto Jesus the author and finisher of our faith; who for the joy that was set before him endured the cross, despising the shame, and is set down at the right hand of the throne of God" (Hebrews 12:2). He's paved the way for us. I see Him there at the finish line, with outstretched arms, beckoning: "Come!" While others sleep, let's keep on running. While others complain, let's keep on running. While others despair, let's keep on running. The finish line is in sight. We will cross!

1) The Legend of Cliff Young, Blog: Running. Health. Education., elitefeet.com

Special Thanks

Thank you to these special people who assisted me in this project:

Nancy Arrowood

Matthew Arrowood

Anna-Leigh Boyd

Tammy Fisher

Iscah Ikerd

Rebekah Mains

Jaredith Mize

Kenny Noble

Samantha Null

Cristy Null

Beth and Robert Pevlor

Additional Books By Larry Monroe Arrowood

God Of Our Fathers

The Shenandoah Series
Book One: Bloodroot
Book Two: The Last Hemlock

Troublesome Blue

Cross Switch

Grace Faith Works, Finding the Biblical Balance
(Revised edition)

They Came to Save Us

Suffering With Purpose
(Revised edition of Surviving the Storm of Suffering)

Overcoming Temptation
(Revised edition)

Building the Home

Books by Larry Arrowood may be ordered through:
Woodsong Publishing
www.woodsongpublishing.com

Or you may order through your preferred bookstore or online outlets such as Barnes and Noble or Amazon

You may contact the author:
www.facebook.com/LarryArrowood
larryarrowood@mac.com

www.ingramcontent.com/pod-product-compliance
Lightning Source LLC
LaVergne TN
LVHW051547070426
835507LV00021B/2449